IMAGES
of Scotland

LINLITHGOW

IMAGES
of Scotland

LINLITHGOW

Compiled by
William F. Hendrie

TEMPUS

First published 1999
Copyright © William F. Hendrie, 1999

Tempus Publishing Limited
The Mill, Brimscombe Port,
Stroud, Gloucestershire, GL5 2QG

ISBN 0 7524 1580 8

Typesetting and origination by
Tempus Publishing Limited
Printed in Great Britain by
Midway Clark Printing, Wiltshire

Contents

Linlithgow is seen spread out below in this aerial photograph of the town. Like most small Scottish towns it used to be largely self-sufficient, producing everything form its own bread to its own beer and whisky. Unlike neighbouring Bo'ness with its coal mines, foundries and saw mills, and Grangemouth with its oil refinery and timber yards, Linlithgow has never been the site of heavy industries. These days its beautiful setting beside Linlithgow Loch has enabled it to develop as a tourist centre and to attract high -tec modern industries such as Californian and Boston based computer firm Sun Micro, and defence specialists Racal.

Acknowledgements

This book looks at many aspects of life in Linlithgow through over 200 photographs, which cover a century from the 1880s to the 1980s. The author would like to thank all of the inhabitants of the town, especially the Revd Ian Paterson, former Provost Jim Shanks and architect Tom Pollock, for providing many of pictures. Thanks also to ex-Provost Shanks, Jimmy Dumbreck MBE and former Linlithgow Primary School janitor and Beadle of St Ninians Craigmaillen church, Bobby Thomson, for information about life in the town in past decades.

Introduction

The Royal and Ancient Burgh of Linlithgow, famous as the birth place of Mary Queen of Scots and for its now ruined royal palace, where she was born in December 1542, attracts thousands of visitors every year. The 'Royal' in Linlithgow's proud title is therefore clearly very well recognised, but less attention is sometimes paid to its equally justified claim to fame as an 'Ancient Burgh'. Many of the pictures in this book are therefore devoted to illustrating Linlithgow's bustling life as one of Scotland's most successful and prosperous country towns.

Linlithgow is believed to mean 'the stretch of water in the damp double hollow' and that graphically describes its situation in the valley between the Bathgate Hills to the south and the Bonnytoun Hills, which separate it from the shores of the River Forth to the north. Way back in geological times, one of the tributaries of the Forth, the River Avon, flowed through this valley and instead of discharging between Grangemouth and Bo'ness as it does today, flowed out close to where Linlithgow's port of Blackness is now situated. It was the last great Scottish Ice Age which changed this pattern and created the scenery around the town as it appears today. As the massive glacier spread slowly south-east from the Highlands it ensheathed the whole area, scraping away the soft layers of sedimentary rock and left its mark in the form of ice striations on the nearby slopes of the Binny Crag to the south-east of the town. It was, however, upon the glacier's eventual retreat as temperatures slowly recovered and rose again, that the Ice Age had its greatest lasting effect upon the area, where Linlithgow was later to grow. As the ice melted it was no longer able to carry the debris which it had acquired along its course and dropped this terminal morain, thus creating the drumlins or small mounds such as Baronshill, which are a marked feature of the eastern approach to the town. At around the same time it appears that an enormous chunk of ice broke off and was left behind to eventually thaw and turn into what is now Linlithgow Loch, with the peninsula on which the royal palace was eventually built in medieval times jutting out into the middle.

It was on the loch that Linlithgow's first inhabitants originally lived, because for defence they occupied crannogs – thatched wooden dwellings built on stilts out in the water and linked to the shore by a cunningly concealed causeway, carefully constructed just below the surface to keep it hidden from enemy attackers. According to local tradition the crannogs were situated near the south shore of the loch in what is now known as Town Bay and centuries later in the middle ages it was here that the burgh's first land based buildings were erected to house the servants for the original royal hunting lodge, which was sited nearby by Scotland's kings, as the peninsula jutting out into the loch provided an easily defendable site.

As well as enabling the monarchs and their courtiers to linger later (while the hunting was good and enjoy a comfortable night's rest), the simple wooden hunting lodge also provided a convenient overnight resting place when the royal retinue journeyed to and from Edinburgh and Stirling Castles. Thus its importance grew and once the stone palace was erected in the latter half of the fifteenth century, many of the Scottish nobles wanted to live as close as possible to all of the action of the royal court. They therefore built their town houses in Linlithgow, where these grander homes added to the steady expansion of the area around the Cross Well and in either direction along the High Street. Amongst the oldest remaining houses are those in Hamilton's Land opposite the post office, which are carefully protected by the National Trust for Scotland under its Little Houses Scheme. Unfortunately, the town houses of the nobles and the homes of the foreign ambassadors who attended the royal court were demolished before conservation became a recognized cause.

By the time of the Union of the Crowns of Scotland and England in 1603, after which the Scottish kings made their homes in London and their visits to Linlithgow became few in number, the Burgh, which had been granted royal status by King Robert II as long ago as 1389, was sufficiently well established to continue to flourish with its many trade guilds ensuring its prosperity. The days when the trade guilds – from the bakers in the Guild of Baxters to the cloth workers in the Guild of Weavers – controlled many aspects of life in Linlithgow, from prices and quality of goods to details of apprenticeships, are still remembered in the town through its Deacons' Court. This is particularly evident on the first Tuesday after the second Thursday in June, when all of the townsfolk are still commanded to attend the annual Riding of the Marches.

The ancient custom of all of the lieges together inspecting the town's marchlands or boundaries was probably undertaken on foot from as early as its creation as a Burgh. The first actual riding on horseback, however, took place towards the end of the reign of King James V, father of Mary Queen of Scots, in the late 1530s, by which time the roads and tracks in the district had been sufficiently improved to make this a practical possibility. What started out as a necessity to preserve the town's assets from encroachment by its neighbours continues to the present day as a pleasurable summer occasion, when Black Bitches from home and abroad gather to show their pride in their hometown.

Among other aspects of their town's past, both men and women are intensely proud to be known as Black Bitches – a nickname derived from the black greyhound bitch on the Burgh's coat of arms. According to legend the greyhound earned its place there by saving the life of her master. She carried food to him when he was wrongfully imprisoned by being chained to the trunk of an oak tree on one of the islands in the loch.

The other famous nickname connected to Linlithgow is Dreamthorp, the title given to the town by well-known Scottish Victorian essayist Alexander Smith. He described Linlithgow as ' a castle, a chapel, a lake, a straggling strip of grey houses with a blue film of smoke over all, lying embossed in emerald. Nothing could be more peaceful. The hands on the clock seem always pointing to one hour. Time has fallen asleep in the afternoon sunshine'.

Linlithgow is still as beautiful as Smith described it, but it has long ago awakened from its 'Brigadoon' like slumber and is now one of the most prosperous, successful bustling small towns in Scotland. Thanks to its ideal situation midway between Edinburgh and Glasgow and its excellent transport links with both cities, the rest of Scotland and south to England, its population has grown from 3,000 at the end of the Second World War to over 15,000 at the Millenium.

Far from regarding their new home merely as a dormitory town, however, the newcomers have shown their appreciation of what Linlithgow has to offer by participating to the full in its many leisure, sports and cultural facilities. These range from its excellent eighteen hole golf course, with a golf range and another course only a couple of miles away, to one of Scotland's most modern swimming pools and sports centres. Other facilities include an arts guild and a top class amateur operatic society. In addition, it has some attractions which other towns cannot offer, such as Scotland's only canal museum and its heritage society, whose permanent exhibition and ever-changing temporary displays at its headquarters in historic Annet House bring the town's past into touch with its present.

One
Around the Cross

The Cross has been the heart of Linlithgow since medieval times . The present elaborately carved three-tiered stone well, topped by the unicorn, which was Scotland's original heraldic beast, was erected in 1806. The intricacies of its sculpted figures, including the town drummer and his accompanying flute player are all the more remarkable as they are the work of stone mason Robert Gray, who was a one-armed veteran of the Napoleonic Wars. He worked with a chisel in his good hand and a mallet attached to the stump of his other arm.

Today the Cross Well is simply an attractive decorative feature in the centre of the town, but originally Linlithgow's wells were a vital feature of daily life as there was no piped water supply and all supplies had thus to be fetched from the public wells situated along the length of the High Street. Other wells, the remains of which can still be seen or whose site is indicated by a place name, included St Michael's Well, Lion Well, Dog Well and New Well. In addition to fetching water, trips to the wells were also an opportunity to gather the latest gossip. Linlithgow is the only town in Scotland with an official town crier and it was always at the Cross Well that he made his announcements, just as he still does on Marches morning. It is also appropriate that for over a century the head office of the local newspaper, the *Linlithgowshire Journal and Gazette*, has been situated on the corner of the High Street overlooking the Cross Well. Its well-read weekly issues, published every Friday, keep the townsfolk up to date with the local news.

Also overlooking the Cross is the Town House, where much of the news used to originate. The present building was completed in 1670, but the earlier Tolbooth stood on this same site for several centuries before that, housing the council chambers where the provost, bailies and councilors held their meetings. The Tolbooth contained the court as well, where the magistrates tried wrongdoers, and the jail to which they could be sent if found guilty. The entrance to the debtors' prison can still be seen at first floor level on the Kirkgate side of the building. On a happier note the Town House and its adjacent Burgh Halls have always been the setting for Linlithgow's social occasions, while amongst its other uses the ground floor also housed the Burgh's first hand hauled fire engine. Later, when the town acquired a horse drawn fire appliance, it was accommodated in a new fire station, where the Coffee Neuk is now situated. More modern motor appliances were also stationed there until traffic congestion around the Cross made this a most unsuitable base. Congestion was always at its worst on market day, which took place in the covered arcade that originally existed at the foot of the Town House and in adjacent Market Lane, where the Masonic Hall is situated. The following pictures illustrate much of the life of events which took place around the Cross in years gone by.

The Town House stands on the site of the former Tolbooth. The original Town House built in 1670 was destroyed by fire in 1847 as the inscription carved on the stonework of the façade recalls. This is how it looked when it was rebuilt, still with its distinctive Italian style piazza stretching the full length of the ground floor. The six covered spaces provided welcome shelter for the stallholders at the weekly market which was held at the Cross. The attractive feature of the piazza remained until 1907 when it was replaced by the now familiar double stairway, designed by architect W. M Scott.

The wooden spire was not restored when the building was rebuilt but was replaced instead with the fine square stone tower seen in this postcard view. Ten years later, in 1857, a public subscription held in the town raised sufficient money to install the clock. Built by Mr MacKenzie, a Glasgow clockmaker, it was the first turret clock constructed in Scotland on the same lines as the famous Westminster Palace clock in London, familiarly known as Big Ben. Through the week the clock is a constant reminder to the reporters of the *Linlithgowshire Gazette* building that their deadline draws ever closer. *The Gazette* was founded on 11 April 1891, and is still owned by F. Johnston and Company, Scotland's largest publisher of local newspapers.

The trusty open-topped Alvis belonging to the *Linlithgowshire Journal and Gazette's* most celebrated editor, Arthur Brown, who was usually known by his nickname of 'Paw Brown'. It is standing next to the statue of the Green Man, waiting to transport him to the scene of the next local story to cover it for that Friday's issue. The car still survives in the possession of his son Henry. 'Paw Brown' also gained fame as a war correspondent. His daughters, Barbara and Iris, are still well-known Linlithgow residents, playing a role in many aspects of the town's life. Barbara was the first woman member of the Deacons' Court. His son-in-law, Tom MacGowran, is former Managing Director of Johnston Newspapers, the group which he served for so many years as editor, and his great grandson Leon is the latest member of the family to follow him into the newspaper industry.

Such a deserted scene at the Cross is hard to imagine nowadays. This view looking to the west is of special interest as it shows the Golden Cross Tavern and other fine historic buildings that were swept away to make room for the modern shops and flats now built incongruously on this prestigious town centre site. Notice the ornate pediment above the window in the corner on the left. The Golden Cross later became a popular tearoom run by Mrs. Holland and Miss Cooper, before these two ladies moved their business across the High Street to open the Charlotte Rooms in the building where the Four Marys Restaurant is now situated.

A noticable feature of the previous two pictures of the Cross is the statue of John Hope, 7th Earl of Hopetoun and Lord Lieutenant, the monarch's representative for Linlithgowshire, as West Lothian was formerly known. This picture shows the huge crowd gathered at the Cross in the year 1911 for the unveiling of the statue, which shows John Hope in all of his Viceroy's finery as Great Britain's first Governor-General of Australia. Hope, whose family live at Scotland's finest stately home, nearby Hopetoun House, also previously enjoyed a celebrated diplomatic career in India. As can be seen from this photograph, there was intense local pride in his international achievements in the days when the British Empire was still held in high esteem in Scotland. Opposite the Cross in Old County Buildings, his famous ancestor, General Sir John Hope, who fought the famous rear-guard action at La Corunna in Spain during the Peninsula Campaign of the Napoleonic War, is also remembered in the fine oil portrait by the celebrated Scottish artist, Henry Raeburn.

The statue of Governor-General Hope was cast in bronze and it discoloured so badly that it was soon nicknamed, 'The Green Man'. Efforts during the 1960s to clean it proved unsuccessful and partly because of this, but mainly because its stone plinth caused a traffic hazard in the days when cars were still allowed to park around the Cross, it was moved in 1970 to its present more secluded site in the Rose Garden, which can be reached from Market Lane or from the Peel. This postcard view was sold by Adam Edgar from his newsagents shop and sub-post office at the Cross. High on top of Erngath Hill, overlooking the Loch at the end of the first fairway of the West Lothian Golf Course, the Hope Monument is dedicated to the memory of another member of the Hope family, Brigadier-General Adrian Hope. Brigadier-General Hope was killed in action in the Indian Mutiny during the attack on Fort Rooeah in 1859.

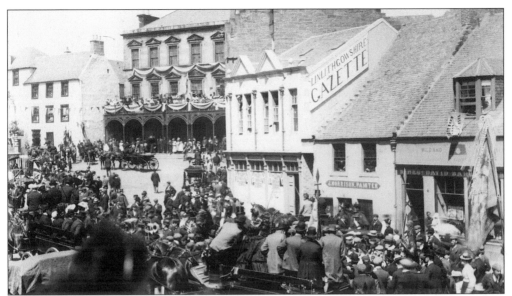

The Cross is always the scene of great activity on Marches morning, as pictured in this fine Edwardian photograph taken before the alterations to the Town House removed the piazza in 1907. Notice the crowd of dignitaries on the decorated balcony above the arches of the wrought iron piazza. The prominent sign on the side of the newspaper offices is a reminder of the days long before the *Linlithgowshire Gazette* incorporated the rival *Bo'ness Journal*. Interestingly, to this day the popular local paper is still known stubbornly and solely as *The Gazette* in Linlithgow and resolutely and simply as *The Journal* in Bo'ness as if the merger never took place!

Sir Winston Churchill visited Linlithgow during his 1945 post-war election tour and is seen here campaigning on the steps of the Town House.

This well-known picture postcard view shows the Cross in the days when the only traffic was horse-drawn. The Black Bitch carved on the Cross Well is the only one in the Royal Burgh depicting the dog facing east. Its head was originally cast in bronze but has been vandalized. On the back of the postcard it is indicated that to post the card in Britain cost one half penny, about a fifth of the modern penny, while to send it overseas cost one old penny. Overseas meant exactly what it stated because, of course, airmail had not yet come into existence. Notice too that the now familiar *Gazette* office had not been constructed when this Victorian view was taken looking east along the High Street, to which we next turn our attention.

Two
Along the High Street

While the Cross has always been the heart of Linlithgow, the High Street has always been its strong backbone, with the lanes, vennels and runrigs running out of it, like sturdy ribs. As a result of its geographic situation in the elongated, narrow valley between the Bathgate Hills to the south and the Bonnytoun Hills to the north, the long High Street from West Port to Low Port and the now largely forgotten East Port, has always been Linlithgow's sole main thoroughfare. The majority of the town's shops are situated along its length and in past centuries, as well as coming there to obtain food and other necessary supplies, the town's inhabitants also had to come every day to fetch their water from its many famous wells. The wells are remembered in the rhyme, 'Glasgow for bells, Linlithgow for wells, Falkirk for pease and brose'.

Victoria Hall and High Street, Linlithgow

This early twentieth-century postcard view shows the Victoria Hall in all of its fine original Scottish baronial style splendour, with its impressive turreted towers.

St Michael's Well still stands on this site at the Low Port end of the High Street, with its inscription 'St Michael is kind to strangers'. This is one of Linlithgow's two proud mottos and one which it truly tries to live up to as it welcomes more and more tourists. An influx of visitors was also expected a century and a half ago with the coming of the railway to Linlithgow on 21 February 1842, when it was predicted that the town would become one of Scotland's new style inland spas. As a result, the eighteenth-century building with its red pantiled roof, seen behind the statue of St Michael in this Victorian view, was demolished to make way for the fine hotel which was erected in 1886 and still occupies the site. It has now been converted into private flats and a shop. St Michael's Well has now been reduced in height as a result of a crash involving a lorry.

Up St Michael's Lane, behind the well in the last picture, was situated the old Mint Tower, where Scotland's currency was produced in the middle ages. It stood close to where the railway station is now situated and as this view, taken shortly before its demolition shows, was a sizeable four-storey building. In medieval times the mint moved from town to town along with the royal court so that the monarch could keep tight personal control on the issue of coinage. Silver was mined in the Bathgate Hills to the south of the town. This view looks north towards the High Street over the roofs of the red pantiled buildings which stood there before the construction of the St Michael's Hotel.

High Street, looking W., Linlithgow

This locally produced Christmas card view captures the days when horse-drawn vehicles were still the only traffic in the High Street. Taken from the Low Port End of the street, the photograph looks west towards the buildings on the far side of the Cross, a century before they were demolished to make way for the present shops and flats.

Prominent on the right are the towers of the Victoria Hall, constructed in 1887 as the town's way of celebrating the golden anniversary of Queen Victoria. The site on the north side of the High Street was gifted by Miss Jessie B. Baird, in memory of her brother, Dr George Dallas Baird, who practised in Linlithgow for fifty years. Designed by Edinburgh architect Mr Russell Walker, the hall, which could seat 800 people including accommodation in the balcony, was completed in 1889 at a cost of £3,800, together with an extra £ 1,500 for the houses and shops on either side, built in the same attractive style. The hall was officially opened on 23 December 1889 by the famous Liberal politician and future prime minister, Lord Rosebery, Lord Lieutenant of Linlithgowshire. He had previously been made a freeman of Linlithgow in 1886. After the Second World War, the hall became the Ritz Cinema and later a bingo hall and amusement arcade. Efforts are still being made to save it form demolition and turn it into the theatre that Linlithgow requires for its Arts Guild and other cultural groups. The sweetie shop to the right of the hall was known as the mile stone shop, as there was a mile stone built into its façade, indicating that it was a mile from there to Gallowsknowe at Linlithgow Bridge, where as the name suggests, public executions by hanging formerly took place.

In the foreground, on the right, is the sign of the Red Lion, one of Linlithgow's most famous hostelries. This coaching inn was originally built in 1625 as a private house by the Kae family. They were well known as Linlithgow's barber surgeons, but as a sideline they were also what were known as the King's Sergeants, which gave them the right to collect taxes. It was when local people came to pay their dues that the building first became a drinking place as the Kaes made extra money by selling them refreshments as they waited their turn. The inn was originally known as the Golden Lion and was the headquarters in the town of the Guild of Hammermen. Why it changed colour is a mystery, but it is suggested that it may simply have been a shortage of gold paint one year at Marches time, when by tradition many frontages in the town are redecorated. Famed for many years for its skittle alley, in 1999 it was converted into an Italian bistro.

17

Another building constructed in distinctly Victorian style in the High Street was the post office, but it was actually not completed until 1904. The post office was previously at the Cross. To make way for its fine new premises, situated conveniently close to the railway station, the old Greenyard cottages and tenement were demolished. The sizeable staff, with the postmaster seated in centre, can be seen posing in front of the new post office that was required as Linlithgow was the sorting office for the entire area. The white board beneath the clock announced postal collection and delivery times and the latest times of posting for guaranteed first delivery in London and towns across the country the following morning.

Four of Linlithgow's postmen wore their uniforms and their military medals with pride when they posed for the photographer for this picture taken shortly after their return to duty after the Armistice in the First World War in November 1918. The postman standing on the right was Willie Harvey, who was also one of the town's halberdiers, and standing on the left was Geordie Oliver, who was also the beadle at St Michael's Kirk. Mail deliveries in those days were made on foot, while urgent telegrams were rushed out by bicycle. Today Linlithgow Post Office, as well as providing local deliveries, is the base for the post bus that carries both mail and passengers to Blackness and the rural Mannerstoun district.

Buses are the prominent mode of travel in this later picture postcard view looking east along the High Street. While the towers and turrets of the Victoria Hall still dominate the scene on the north side of the street, the tower of the bank building is prominent on the south side. Constructed originally in 1859 as the Commercial Bank of Scotland, the bank's premises were deliberately designed to look like a castle, complete with stone tower and fortified with imitation cannon as a very visible signal to local investors of its security and solidarity.

The Four Marys restaurant and bar is well known for its range of real ales and its gantry of Scottish malts. Originally, however, before it dispensed good food and drinks, this building dispensed medicines because it was one of two premises in the High Street owned by Spence the Chemist. The Spence family also ran a newsagents with a printing press behind the building, while upstairs on the first floor they had a toy shop. At an earlier date the chemist's business was operated by the distinguished pharmacist David Waldie. Later in his career, Waldie pioneered the use of anaesthetics in surgery by being the first to propose to Sir James Young Simpson that he experiment with the use of chloroform. The plaque above the entrance to the Four Marys gives details of the Linlithgow chemist's noteworthy career, which took him south to England and as far afield as India. (Photograph by kind permission of John Doherty)

19

John Braes operated a licensed grocers at 182 High Street. Here, the proprietor poses with his staff at the entrance, flanked by large double windows that were crowded with displays of the range of products on sale, from teas to wine. In order that customers did not have to carry baskets full of purchases up Linlithgow's steep hills, Braes operated a delivery service and many customers had weekly standing orders. Later the shop was converted into a cloth merchants by Mick Devine, whose daughter Nora still continues in business in the town with her well-known wool shop. The shop next door beyond the pend was Dalrymple's chip shop.

George Gillespie's shop at 68 High Street stood on the site now occupied by Boots the Chemist and formerly by Veitch's menswear shop. Like Brae's grocery, it is noted in the Linlithgow Business Directory for 1895. Mr Gillespie maintained Linlithgow's proud connection with the leather industry, the town at one time being in Scotland second only to Perth in the manufacture of leather products. Gillespie's range of goods included all of the harness and tracery required by local farmers. He was also patronized by local teachers, as his school punishment straps rivaled the Lochgelly tawse for the searing sting which they could effectively deliver to miscreant pupils without inflictiing any lasting harm. Later Gillespies was taken over by Hebsons, and pupils of St Josephs Primary in the early 1920s recall that it was the source of headmistress Miss Hobin's bamboo canes, before her successor in 1927, Mr William Hall, although English, changed the school's mode of chastisement to the Scottish tawse. On a more cheerful note, when the shop was still a saddlery, boys often made their way up the stairs to the first floor where saddler Alex Geoch blew up and laced their leather footballs for tuppence – or for free if in an especially good mood!

Another place in Linlithgow where corporal punishment was meted out to juvenile wrongdoers was the Sheriff Court. The stern Victorian façade is shown in this nineteenth century photograph, and it is intriguing to wonder whether the mischievous baker's messenger boy with his tray of morning rolls on his head ever suffered the punishment of the birch rod! Linlithgow's burgh jail was originally housed in the Town House, where punishments also included scourging with the leather lash and branding with the Linlithgow brand, an iron capital 'L'. Sentences of capital punishment were also passed by the court and the last public hanging took place at the Cross in 1857. Bathgate labourer John McLean was put to death for killing a man in a brawl at Boghead Bridge on the road to Armadale. His last breakfast was carried to him by a waitress from the Bluebell Café. By coincidence, Linlithgow's most famous murder, and the first committed in Scotland using a hand-held gun, took place in front of where the Sheriff Court building stands in 1570, when Mary Queen of Scots' half brother, James Stewart, Earl of Moray, was assassinated by James Hamilton of Bothwell.

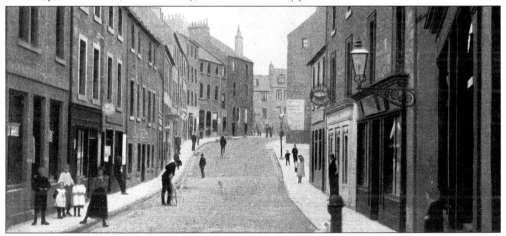

All the buildings on the left in this very early postcard view were sadly demolished in the 1960s, when the town councillors of the day replaced them with the modern Vennel flats. The name is derived from the French verb *venir* meaning 'to come', and is a reminder of the French influence on life in Scotland in the middle ages. The shop below the street lamp was known as the River Plate, because it sold frozen meat and tins of corned beef from the Argentine. The Spanish Ambassador's House can be seen on the left, while the Union Bank was also sited in this part of the High Street.

This early photograph of the newly completed Vennel flats shows the planned view of St Michael's and Linlithgow Palace, which the architects designed to be an exciting vista from the High Street. It has been lost, however, because of the planting of trees which have a preservation order that prevents them from being lopped. This picture captures the stark contrast between the historic and the modern and perhaps helps explain why the Vennel development was presented with a Saltire Award in 1969.

This Victorian postcard picture shows the High Street looking in the other direction from the Vennel to the west. On the right is the Buttercup dairy, King the jeweller, the Gospel Hall in whose worship Mr Veitch the lawyer played a leading role, Alan's radio shop and Willie 'Shiny' Meek's shoe shop. Mr Meek was the brother of Gladys Meek, Linlithgow Academy's renowned French teacher. In the far distance is Oliphants bakers shop, which has served Linlithgow with its morning rolls, lunchtime mutton pies and afternoon cream cakes for well over a century. The Vennel, which runs at the side of Oliphants bakehouse, still bears signs of Linlithgow's leather industry, with iron runners to slide the heavy bales of hides to the tannery that stood on the shores of the loch whose waters were so essential in the tanning process. While leather making no longer takes place in Linlithgow, craftsmen still ply their trade in this part of the town with a glaziers and Mannerstoun antiques and restorers having premises in this area.

Three
The West Port

The West Port, as the name derived from the French word for door indicates, used to be the site of the west gate into the town. The gate was opened at dawn and closed at dusk. Time for its closure was indicated by the sounding of the curfew, the order in French to *couvre le feu*, 'cover the fire', so that the inhabitants might do just that. They could then fall asleep in their beds knowing that they and their homes were safe both from fire and from enemy intruders. At one time in the 1600s, when plague broke out in Bo'ness because of the new ports failure to impose strict quarantine regulations, the magistrates of Linlithgow gave orders that a gallows be erected at West Port so that if any Bo'nessian was rash enough to venture over the Flints, the high hill between the two towns, he could be made to pay for his intrusion by jouking the gibbet! Even in less stressful periods, the fact that the big solid wooden gates were often still shut when the travellers arrived, gave rise to the establishment of several inns and pubs in this part of the town. The oldest of them is the well-known Black Bitch, named after Linlithgow's legendary greyhound, which is depicted on its sign. Originally, however, the sign for the Black Bitch was a butcher's wooden slab with a sharp-bladed knife and a large cleaver painted on it, to indicate that it was the headquarters of the town's Guild of Fleshers. The Black Bitch still plies a busy trade as does the West Port Hotel next door, but the Customs House Inn, which stood on the corner of St Ninian's Road leading out of the town to Bo'ness, has long been demolished

Katie Wearie's Tree has for centuries been a feature of the scene at West Port. It is said to have taken its unusual name from a female cattle drover who often paused to enjoy a wee rest in the shade of its branches while on her way to and from market. In this Victorian postcard picture a horse enjoys a drink at the horse trough which used to be situated below the tree. It is claimed that it was seen as a sign of their manhood when laddies attending Linlithgow Public School were able safely to jump the width of the horse trough without falling in and getting 'drookit'.

Some of the pupils of Linlithgow Public School can be seen in this Victorian picture postcard view, standing and sitting in the sun under the famous tree. The shop on the corner of Preston Road, known as Mary Meikle's Corner, was for long the tuck shop, where pupils from the school stopped on their way to and from classes to buy sweeties, lollipops and bars of chocolate. During its later years the wee shop was run by Billy Gray and his wife Jean. Preston Road takes its name from the priests who used to use it as a route to reach their farm at the top of the hill and as a route to the Carmelite Friary of the White Fathers at Nether Parkley. The Friary was founded in 1290 and dedicated to the Virgin Mary.

This photograph shows the famous Katie Wearie's tree after it was struck by lightening. Behind it can be seen the original infant building of Linlithgow Public School, which was known affectionately as 'The Wee Public'. The school was founded in 1844, following the Disruption of the Church of Scotland in the previous year, by members of the town's newly formed Free Kirk. In the background, behind the blackened stump of Katie Wearie's Tree, can be seen St Ninian's parish church, which was to be eventually reunited with Craigmaillen Free Kirk.

The lofty steeple of St Ninian's Craigmaillen parish church is a well-known landmark at West Port. Belonging to the Church of Scotland, St Ninian's lives in the shadow of the magnificent St Michael's, but is itself a very fine example of Scottish Victorian architecture with its spacious stone nave, chancel, choir and apse. Its minister is the Revd Ian Morrison, and since the 1970s it has been lovingly looked after by its well-known beadle, Bobby Thomson, who was formerly manager of Bo'ness Co-operative Society's Peel House headquarters, now converted into the town's medical centre.

Katie Wearie's Tree fortunately survived the lightening strike and this attractive picture postcard photograph shows the young sprouts growing out of the blackened tree trunk. Behind can be seen the infant classrooms of Linlithgow Public School and the site is still the West Port annexe of Linlithgow Primary. Also in the background is the grey sandstone building of St Ninian's Craigmaillen church with its slate roof and tall spire. Opposite the tree are the premises of the West Port Hotel, where for many years the famous John McKay was the almost legendary mine host, and its dining room offered the game which his son Iain loved to shoot. After being run more recently by well-known former footballer and Linlithgow Rose manager Colin Sinclair, the hotel, which now also offers the spacious Palace Suite, is currently owned by Alloa Brewery. The West Port was originally a coaching inn. Where the car park is now situated to the west of the hotel was the site of the town's Horse Head Market, where as well as being bought and sold, horses could also be hired.

West Port House is Linlithgow's oldest occupied home. Now converted into modern apartment homes, according to tradition it was at one time the home of Mary of Guise, Mary Queen of Scot's mother, when as Queen Mother she became Regent of Scotland during the minority of her grandson King James VI of Scotland and I of Great Britain.

Four
Kirk, Peel and Palace

From the High Street and the Cross, the steep Kirk Gate leads up the hill to St Michael's church, the ruins of the royal palace and the Peel, the beautiful royal park within which they stand. Although there is indeed a gate at the top it in the shape of the New Entry which King James V had constructed to give more convenient access to the palace, it is probable that the Kirk Gate is misspelt and should actually be written Kirk Gait. Gait means stride and this spelling is found in many Scandinavian street names as well as in the term the Lang Gait, which was the original name for Edinburgh's Princes Street in the early eighteenth century when it was simply a country track along the north shore of the Nor' Loch. A similar use of the word Gait, although now spelt gate, is also found in York as is also the case in many Scandinavian cities. The Peel, too, has an interesting derivation, coming probably from a Norman French word for a sharp pointed piece of wood from which the fence surrounding such a royal park was constructed. This same source also gave us the term 'peel tower' for a simple, square-shaped, stone-built Scottish castle. There is also the well-known saying 'To be beyond the pale'. This meant that the manners of anyone living outside the bounds of the royal domain were considered uncouth and is said to come from the fence which originally surrounded the city of Dublin. Nowadays there are two royal parks in Scotland – at Holyrood and in Linlithgow – and they share the distinction of being guarded by their own royal constabulary. Traditionally the policeman at the Peel is known appropriately as 'The Peelie'. The magnificent sweeping parkland, which he protects and whose gates he locks and unlocks every night and morning, is believed to have been one of the first places in Scotland where the game of golf was played, one of the first participants being Mary Queen of Scots. Mary was born at the palace on a cold winter day in December 1542. A horseman galloped to Fife to relay the news to her father James V, who lay dying at Falkland Palace. 'It cam' wi a lass and it'll gang wi' a lass', are said to have been his dying words, meaning that the Scottish royal house of Stewart had gained the throne through the marriage of King Robert the Bruce's daughter, Princess Marjory, to Walter, her Lord High Steward, and would now lose it through the inability of his baby daughter to control the Scottish nobles. Mary's controversial life and death have certainly put Linlithgow Palace on the world tourist map, but the ruined building which they explore has actually more connections with King James IV and his young English Tudor bride, Princess Margaret, during whose reign the palace was nearing completion, and within whose thick stone walls they loved to holiday. Despite Margaret's close connections with Linlithgow, it is a carving of the earlier Scottish Queen Margaret, wife of King Malcolm Canmore, which visitors find on the magnificent pulpit of neighbouring St Michael's kirk. This and other treasures of this historic parish church are well illustrated by the photographs which follow.

This harvest scene, which appears to have been painted looking west from Linlithgow's Burgh Muir, shows the towers of the town's unique trio of historic buildings. From left to right: the slender wooden spire of the Town House, the tall stone spire of St Michael's Kirk and those of the royal palace. It is interesting to note the large number of women at work in the field, bringing home the harvest.

From the ruined, roofless state of Linlithgow Palace, this rural view was clearly painted after 1746. The palace was destroyed by fire after the government Red Coats, under their much hated commander the Duke of Cumberland, departed in haste to pursue the Jacobites. They either carelessly or deliberately failed to extinguish the huge bonfire which they had built to keep them warm when they sheltered in the palace for the night on 31 January 1746. The building was gutted by the blaze, which the next issue of the *Scots Magazine* reported had been seen from as far away as Edinburgh. It has never been restored or re-roofed but after much careful consideration the officials of its present guardians, Historic Scotland, are studying ambitious plans to replace the roof on the north wing. The latest part of the palace to be built, when it was reconstructed following the royal visit of King James in 1617, its five storeys (four of them of guest bedrooms), is seen clearly framed by the trees in this painting. During the seventeenth century the Keeper of the Palace and his family had their private accommodation on the top floor of this side of the palace in a historic version of the modern penthouse suite. Before leaving this attractive picture, notice that the artist also gave great prominence to the intricate stone crown atop St Michael's. He also appears to have taken some licence with the siting of the Town House spire.

Cockleroi, Linlithgow's well known hill, looms out of all proportion in this eighteenth century painting of the loch and palace, looking to the west. Cockleroi is said to derive its unusual name from the French court influence in Linlithgow and to mean, 'the cockaded hat of the king'. Today there is a car park at its foot and it is an easy walk to the summit, which is an excellent viewpoint from where it is possible to look out right across the narrow waist of Central Scotland from the Bass Rock jutting out of the Forth. On the clearest of days even the May Island at the river's mouth in the east and the peaks of the Sleeping Warrior on Arran in the Clyde to the west can be seen. To the north-west, lookout for the Ochils and Ben Ledi towering above the entrance to the Trossachs.

This famous Slezer print of Linlithgow looking from the other direction – from the west, where St Ninian's Road runs today – shows Cockleroi more to scale, rising to the south behind the town. Of particular interest is Slezer's view of the Peel, which, if he drew it accurately, gave the palace a decidedly wedding cake appearance. It also provides a splendid picture of St Michael's Kirk and, at the foot of the Kirk Gate, the towering spire of the Town House and the houses spread out along the length of the High Street behind the shores of the loch.

The same outlook is seen in this 1930s picture postcard view showing the swans on the loch. Linlithgow Loch is a bird sanctuary, but in the middle ages, at banquets in the palace, roast swan took the place of the peacocks served as the centre piece at English Tudor feasts. The swan was carefully plucked before it was roasted. After it was cooked, the feathers were stuck on again and then, with wings and neck outstretched it was carried high by the servants along the entire length of the huge banqueting hall to be presented to the King and Queen. The King and Queen were seated on their dias at the top table in front of Scotland's largest fireplace, where whole tree trunks were burnt to keep them warm throughout the evening. When the path round the shore of the loch was constructed in the 1930s, owners of the long garden riggs, which ran right down to the edge of the water, refused to allow it to cross their land. It had therefore to be built out into the water.

31

Boating on the loch has always been a popular activity as shown by these boys having fun in this Edwardian postcard view taken by local photographer C.M. Spence. Nowadays children can learn to sail properly by attending the many excellent water sports courses run by fully qualified outdoor education instructors at West Lothian Council's residential Low Port Centre at the east end of the loch. Notice St Michael's without its crown.

This scene of boating on the loch in the 1920s shows the lawns of the Peel and the palace, 'bossomed high in tufted trees', as seen from the east, where Low Port Outdoor Education Centre is situated on its shores.

This unusual Victorian print shows the stone crowned tower of St Michael's, with the arched gateway of the sixteenth-century New Outer Entry below and the ruins of the palace in the background.

The fine stone crown of St Michael's Kirk, demolished in 1821 because it was feared that it was too heavy for the church's tower, is seen in detail in this print.

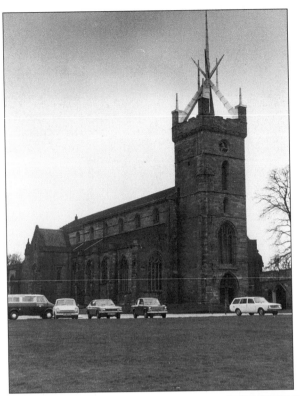

For almost a century and a half, St Michael's was bereft of its spire, until in the early 1960s its well-known minister and one-time Moderator of the Church of Scotland, the Very Revd Dr David Steel, decided that it should be replaced, not with another stone crown but with an ultra-modern one, constructed by contemporary craftsmen using space-age materials. The result in 1964 was the Crown of Thorns, which was erected in the same year. Built of prelaminated timber obtained form Muirheads of Grangemouth and clad in aluminium so that it will never lose its golden gleam and never tarnish, it has been a controversial feature of the Linlithgow townscape ever since. (Photograph by kind permission of John Doherty)

Its critics have described it as a misguided space missile, poised to take off at any minute, while others have asked when it is going to be finished, but the starkly modern Crown of Thorns on top of St Michael's also has its admirers. They point out that Dr Steel's daring decision has truly put Linlithgow on the map, as all who travel on the main railway line from Edinburgh to Glasgow or pass through the town on the M9 motorway certainly recognize the town as a result of the controversial spire. (Photograph by kind permission of John Doherty)

Seated in the palace forecourt outside the church on one of the prelaminated pieces that was hoisted to the top of he tower of St Michael's to build the Crown of Thorns, the men of the construction team pose for the camera. The team consisted of from left to right: T. Reynolds (Mason), P. Haynes, J. Fisher, J. Girdler, G. Hogg, T. Burnet and A. Sutherland (Erection Squad). Three other masons who worked on the project were J. Hutchison, J. Barrie and J. Kielner. The erection of the Crown was supervised by Colin MacAndrew and Partners Ltd, Edinburgh.

Despite adverse weather conditions, the men entrusted with the erection of the Crown of Thorns completed the job on time and each received a £20 bonus for doing so. The scaffolding, however, which surrounded the tower of St. Michael's during the restoration work that took place at the same time, was still in place when the man behind all the furore, the Very Revd David Steel, welcomed that year's Moderator of the Church of Scotland, the Right Revd Duncan Fraser, to conduct the service of rededication of the historic Kirk.

While the controversy raged, Dr Steel enjoyed the peace and quiet afforded by his favourite sport of fishing. His son David, as leader of the Liberal Party, was later to stir up many more rows, especially over his forthright support for abortion.

As the winter winds stripped the trees in the graveyard of St. Michael's of their leaves, the scaffolding came down to reveal the Crown of Thorns. Some admired its eye-catching beauty and praised the stark simplicity of its clean-cut lines, but others could not accept the incongruity of using such modern materials in such a historic setting. Placed elsewhere they declared the Crown of Thorns might be acceptable as a piece of modern art, but definitely not on top of their beloved St Michael's! The row raged on not only in Linlithgow but in the columns of the national press, where reaction was equally mixed. A third of a century later the Crown of Thorns has defied many of its critics by surviving the ravages of the weather and is still a talking point with the ever-increasing number of visitors who come to Linlithgow each year. (Photograph by kind permission of John Doherty)

Dr Steel's successor, the Revd Ian Paterson, is pictured here at his induction in 1977. Born in Ayr in 1938, he was educated at Ayr Academy and Glasgow University. After graduating with the degrees of MA and BD, Mr Paterson spent a year in the USA at the Union Theological Seminary in New York. After completion of his studies he continued his foreign travels, becoming a minister in the Presbyterian Church in East Africa, where he served from 1964 to 1972, the final four years at St Andrew's, Nairobi, where Dr Steel had also been minister. Upon his return to Scotland, Mr Paterson became Chaplain to Stirling University, where he met his future wife Lorna, who was at the time Depute Registrar, before later becoming General Secretary of the Church of Scotland's Woman's Guild, a post which she held until her retirement in 1998. During his time in Linlithgow, Mr Paterson has been honoured by being appointed as one of Her Majesty the Queen's chaplains, and has preached at Crathies as well as having the opportunity of welcoming Her Majesty to St Michael's.

Minister at St Michael's for over thirty years, the Revd Ian Paterson looks on as Her Majesty, Queen Elizabeth is introduced to one of the church's elders, session clerk Derek Henderson, watched by his wife, Margaret. Her Majesty visited the church in July 1989 and later attended the service of dedication for the beautifully refurbished Queen's Aisle, unveiling a plaque to mark the occasion. Designed by well-known local architect and member of the congregation of St Michael's, Mr William Cadell of the house of Grange, the Queen's Aisle provides an intimate space within the old kirk for those seeking peace to pray and for services involving smaller numbers of worshippers. All of the furniture and furnishings have been made by local craftsmen, and an especially pleasing feature is the use of tinted glass, recalling the famous ladder rainbow window in the Royal Presence Chamber in the nearby palace. The small organ in the Queen's Chapel was gifted to the church by the local Masonic Lodge, Ancient Brazen Number Seventeen, one of the oldest in the world. Free Masonry has flourished in Linlithgow for over 350 years and the poet Robert Burns attended a meeting of the local lodge.

On an earlier royal visit to St Michael's in the 1930s, a large crowd of Linlithgow people looked on as Her Majesty Queen Mary, Queen Elizabeth's grandmother, shook hands with the church's minister, the Revd Dr Cooper, on the west steps of the Kirk. It was here in the early sixteenth century that King James IV, every year at Easter, presided over the ceremony of the Skire Siller, Scotland's equivalent of the distribution of Maundy Money. In addition to handing out coins to the beggars and paupers who made their way up the Kirk Gate to St Michael's, King James also washed their feet in remembrance of the actions of Christ at the Last Supper. Before they departed, he handed them new clothes and wooden bowls and platters from which to eat their food during the coming year.

A further photograph from the archives of St Michael's church shows elders Lord Clydesmuir on the left and Robert Crichton, chief executive of Scottish Oils, on the right. They are about to distribute the elements to the congregation at a communion sevice conducted by the Revd David Steel shortly after the dedication of the magnificently carved communion stalls in 1955. Others in the picture include, at the holy table, elders John Brock on the right and Wilson Connor on the left and, seated in the background, assistant minister the Revd Mr Brown. Against the wall on the left are elders John Dickson and James Flett. James Flett was the town's burgh surveyor.

The interior of St Michael's looked much more cluttered before the removal of the side galleries. The central pulpit with its surrounding railings and the box pews are in the foreground, but the eye-catching Creation window in the apse still dominates the scene. This spectacularly beautiful large stained glass window is dedicated to the memory of Sir Charles Wyville Thomson, leader of the famous Challenger Expedition, which in Victorian times between the years 1872 and 1876 sailed over 70,000 miles, revealing many hitherto unknown details about the world's ocean bed. Appropriately the Creation window starts at the top with the heavens and descends through man and beasts on the earth to the depths of the sea, with details showing a spouting whale and the fin of a shark.

The interior of St Michael's as it appeared after it was renovated, looking from the west door down the nave through the chancel and choir to the apse. Notice the paraffin lamps. The fact that St Michael's has the Arch Angel as its patron saint is believed to indicate that it stands on the site of a very early religious victory in Scotland and that worship has taken place on this hill top site overlooking the loch since the earliest of Christian times. The present building was dedicated in 1242 by Bishop de Bernham of St Andrew's, in whose diocese St Michael's was situated and of which it was originally a daughter church. The places where the Bishop sprinkled the holy water as he blessed the church can still be identified as they were marked with consecration crosses carved in the stonework of the walls. Some of the crosses are misleading, however, as several stones have been moved over the years during renovation work on this historic kirk where Scotland's Kings and Queens worshipped regularly for several centuries. While examining the walls, notice the stone seat which runs round them. It is a reminder of the days when there were no pews as worshippers stood throughout the saying of the Mass unless unfit to do so, in which case they brought their own folding stools, like the famous Jenny Geddes in St Giles in Edinburgh, or sat at the side on this stone seat. This gave rise to the saying, 'Let the weak go to the wall', of which the nearest modern equivalent is probably the Americanism, 'If you can't stand the heat, get out of the kitchen'.

The intricately carved stone font in St Michael's still stands at the rear of the Kirk, just inside the West Door, the traditional site of the baptistry. This is a reminder of the days when the church was a Roman Catholic place of worship and it was customary for babies to be blessed with their Christian name before entering the actual body of the Kirk. The bronze interior of the font is carved with a fish, a reminder of the early Christian sign used among the faithful in times of persecution when it was too dangerous to openly make the sign of the cross. The window behind the font occupies the site of the original leper squint – the slanting window through which sufferers from this dreaded skin disease could peer in to see all that was taking place at the high altar. Thus, they could take part in the worship without themselves entering the building and risking infecting other member of the congregation. The window is used to display the church's beautiful communion vessels and plate. The circular alms plate was given to the church by Her Majesty Queen Elizabeth. (Photograph by kind permission of John Doherty)

One of St Michael's most famous features is its bells. As this picture shows, there are three of them. The oldest bell bears the inscription 'The town of Linlithgow made me in the reign of the august Lord James IV,' and as was the custom was installed in 1481 to indicate that the main work of building the church was at last completed. Again following tradition, the bell was named 'St Michael' in honour of the church's patronal saint. By the eighteenth century, 'St Michael' became cracked and, in 1773, the Town Councilors of Linlithgow requested the Burgh Treasurer to obtain costs from Edinburgh for its repair. At the next meeting he reported back that no foundry in Edinburgh could tackle the job, and in the end St Michael was shipped from Bo'ness to London to specialist bell founders, Peck and Chapman. They recast it and added the Burgh coat of arms and the date, before sending it back aboard the *Samuel and Jean* to be reinstalled in the belfry above the West Door at St Michael's. In comparison with 'St Michael' the second bell to be installed, 'Ave Maria', has led an uneventful life, never leaving her lofty perch high above Linlithgow.

This photograph of the Kirk Gate shows the home of Wee Meg Duncan, who in her day was a very 'weel kent figure' in this part of Linlithgow. On Sunday mornings she habitually stationed herself outside her house and soundly chided any latecomers hastening up the hill for the service at St Michael's. Her warnings of the ire of the minister, which their late arrival in the pews would provoke, and the sharpness of her tongue became notorious amongst the worshippers. Appropriately, when the third and smallest of the church bells was installed and found to have a sharper tone than its larger partners, they dubbed it 'Wee Meg Duncan', and by this nickname it is known to the present day. During the 1950s Meg's former home became a sweetie shop and more recently has been the site of St Michael's Church Lighthouse Book Shop.

The innermost sanctum of St Michael's, the apse, is one of the most beautiful parts of what must surely rank as the most magnificent parish church in Scotland. In this picture the vases of Easter lilies frame the holy table, behind which can be seen the intricate carving above the communion stalls and reredos, a splendid 1950s addition displaying the best of modern Scottish craftsmanship. The carpet was specially woven for St Michael's by Templetons of Glasgow and is described in more detail in the following captions.

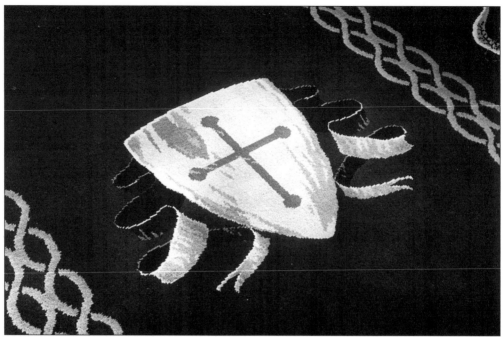

The carpet in the choir and the apse is a unique design depicting the distinctive St Michael's Cross, whose bars are capped by four golden balls. The crosses on the carpet are surrounded by a never-ending Celtic eternity chain.

The carpet, which the craftsmen who hand-wove it at Templetons, overlooking Glasgow Green, assured the church will actually improve in quality with age, also bears the motif of the dragon which was slain by St. Michael, with his lance piercing its steely blue eye as it breathes the last of its vivid flames.

St Michael is shown, spear in hand, in this carving above the communion stalls. In contrast below him is the dove of peace. St Michael's is indeed a veritable Noah's Ark of a church with a menagerie of creatures both real and legendary to be discovered. Look out for instance for carvings of a cheeky little monkey and a wee green puddock. One bird missing from the collection is the cockerel, which looked out over the town as the church's weathervane from 1769 until the demolition of its stone crown in 1821. Made of lead it is however still preserved in the Linlithgow Heritage Exhibition at Annet House in the High Street. Sadly its predecessor has not survived. It would have been of particular interest as a description of it states that it was erected as long ago as the reign of King James III and consisted not of the usual cock but of a mother hen followed by her brood of chickens. It also bore the monarch's favourite motto, 'Ever Watchful', inscribed along its base. It was blown down in a late winter gale in 1768, which also damaged the stone crown of the church.

Mary Queen of Scots is one of three monarchs whose intricately carved wooden statuettes adorn the niches of the famous Queens Pulpit in St Michael's. The others are the eleventh-century Queen Margaret, wife of King Malcolm Canmore, and Queen Victoria. One space remains and it is a matter of speculation whether it will be filled by a carving of the much-beloved Queen Elizabeth, the Queen Mother, or of our present monarch, who has twice visited St Michael's and allowed her name to be given to the Queen's Aisle. (Photograph by kind permission of John Doherty)

Mary Queen of Scots is Linlithgow's most famous Black Bitch. Her first days were spent at Linlithgow, where she was baptised either in the Chapel Royal within the palace or more probably across the palace forecourt in St Michael's before being removed to Stirling Castle and then the island priory on Inchmahome in the middle of the Lake of Menteith to keep her safe from the 'Rough Wooing' of the English. Mary paid three other visits to Linlithgow that were of particular significance. In 1565 the 6' 1" tall, red-haired Queen Mary and her second husband, her cousin Henry, Lord Darnley, stayed at the palace while marching to Glasgow to suppress the uprising of the Protestant Lords. In 1567 she spent her last night with Darnley at Linlithgow, and before the following evening he was mysteriously killed at Kirk o' Field House in Edinburgh. Finally, later that year on 23 April, Mary stayed at the palace on the night before her welcomed pre-arranged abduction by Lord Bothwell on her journey back to Edinburgh. Mary later fled to England where she was held captive by her cousin Queen Elizabeth, until she was executed in 1587.

The Boy Samuel window in the Celtic Chapel is the smallest, but one of the most loved, stained-glass windows in St Michael's. It was installed in this position by the church's former minister and historian, the Revd Dr Ferguson, so that every time he looked up from preaching he would be reminded of his little daughter Esther who lost her life when her hair was being dried in front of the fire in the manse (then situated at the top of Manse Road). Sadly, Esther's older sister also died in tragic circumstances when she and her fiance, the Town Clerk's son, were both drowned after crashing through the ice while skating on the loch. With its rich colours, the Boy Samuel window has been a popular choice for reproduction as a Christmas card, but St Michael's also has a charming nativity window of its own. (Photograph by John Doherty)

Bringing the nativity scene to life were these young parishioners of St Michael's of a previous generation. The church's fine pipe organ, recently restored, can be glimpsed in the background.

Another Christmas custom at St Michael's is the gathering of gifts by the children of the congregation to donate to youngsters who are experiencing a less than happy childhood. In this picture taken around the year 1980 are, from left to right: Shona Peters, Fraser Meldrum, Russell Eadie and his young sister Lesley Eadie. They are presenting parcels to Mrs Young, representing the Scottish Society of the Prevention of Cruelty to Children, which has since become known as Children First.

St Michael is also portrayed in by a stained-glass window in the Queen's Aisle of the kirk, depicting the history of the building of the church with illustrations of how it looked down through the ages until Queen Victoria's reign. The motto connected with the patronal saint is, 'May the might of St Michael establish us in the heavens'.

Outside too, St Michael is depicted, but this time with his wings clipped as a result of an attack on him by the Rascal Multitude at the time of the Reformation in 1560. This angry mob felt that all statues on churches were idolatrous reminders of the Catholic church and succeeded in smashing all of the other statues of the saints, both in St Michael's and the Chapel Royal within the palace, despite the strong condemnation of Protestant leader John Knox. St Michael himself, however, was so securely built into the fabric of the Kirk that all of their efforts failed to dislodge him. Although knocked about more than a wee bit, he happily survives as the patronal saint who looks down upon all of the church's many visitors. Behind can be seen the castellations of the battlements incorporated into the building of St Michael's during the reign of the English King Edward I. Living up to his reputation as the 'Hammer of the Scots', he occupied Linlithgow Palace as his headquarters in 1305, and incorporated the church into his defences. Interestingly, the battlements are only on the side overlooking the town from which any attack might have been expected to come.

Masons exercised their skilled craft on the stone work of St Michael's during the restoration work done during the early 1950s. Further extensive preservation work during the 1990s has prepared St Michael's for the new millenium.

The Very Revd David Steel leads the Moderator of the Church of Scotland, the Right Revd Leonard Small, out of the South Door of St Michael's on a blustery day. The South Porch was where many marriages were conducted in the days when the church was very strict about those who were allowed to wed within its actual interior. Look up and you will find a wedding ring carved in the stone of the porch's vaulted ceiling . The pauper's coffin, with its sliding bottom so that it could be used over again, was stored in the room above the South Porch.

The South Porch is seen clearly in this 1950s picture postcard view, taken from the peaceful retreat of the Rose Garden. The Rose Garden is situated on the site of the old Burgh Grammar School, whose pupils are said to have taken a delight in utilizing the skulls which were washed down on days of heavy rain from the graveyard above into their playground, to play football. The town's curling rink was situated at the upper entrance to the Rose Garden, where there were spaces in the stone wall for the storage of the granite curling stones.

Bringing to life another incident in the colourful history of Linlithgow, members of the town's Festival Trust re-enact the welcome given to Prince Charles Edward Stuart, Bonnie Prince Charlie, the Young Pretender, when he visited Linlithgow Palace in 1745 on his triumphant march south to Edinburgh. The re-enactment in the courtyard of the palace is presented on Sunday afternoons in August.

Opposite: The churchyard is well worth a visit to browse amongst tombstones and learn form the inscriptions about the lives and businesses of those townsfolk of Linlithgow from past generations who lie buried there. Still preserved there are the two heavy cast iron mortsafes, which used to be placed over every new grave for a period of three weeks to try to discourage the attention of the infamous 'resurrectionists'. These body snatchers got good money for every fresh body they stole and rushed overnight to present in the morning to Dr Knox, the Professor of Anatomy at the Univeristy of Edinburgh. The two most famous of the body snatchers, Burke and Hare, both stayed in Linlithgow around the year 1820, while working as 'navvies' (the labourers employed to dig the Union Canal).

The junior palace guides from Linlithgow Primary School also often help to publicize the town's historic past. Here Andrew Selkirk, Lindsay Gibson and Fiona MacFarlane help advertise the re-enactment at the Peel of the Battle of the Nations (see also picture on page 54).

The ancient stonework of the outer archway of the New Entry was lined with wood to protect it from damage from contractors' lorries when this photograph was taken of it during the 1970s. The Outer Yett, as it is also known, was constructed in the sixteenth century during the reign of King James V, father of Mary Queen of Scots. James is famed as the people's king, who loved to roam freely amongst his subjects disguised as the 'Guid Man o' Ballenguich'. He had the New Entry built at Linlithgow to bring the palace and the nobles of the Royal Court into closer contact with the townsfolk of Linlithgow. The entrance on the south side of the palace was also constructed at this time to replace the former main entrance, the gateway of which can still of seen on the east façade. While James may be regarded as a particularly humble and very human monarch, he was still sufficiently proud to decorate the outer arch of the New Entry with the heraldic shields of the many orders of which he was a member. They are detailed in the following four captions.

First on the left is the Order of the Garter, the highest of the English orders and still in the personal possession of Her Majesty Queen Elizabeth. Under the English crown, it depicts St George slaying the dragon. There are many lions in heraldry, such as the lion couchant (lying flat on its stomach with head raised), the lion statant (standing on all four legs) and the lion rampant (rearing up on its left hind leg). Here the English lion passant guardant (walking towards the left and turning to face the viewer) is depicted three times, while the national flower of England, the Tudor Rose, is carved eight times in the surrounding gold chain.

The much fiercer Scottish lion rampant is seen in all its ferocious glory on the second shield, which represents the Order of St Andrew, invented by James V and awarded to himself. It later became the Order of the Thistle, which like that of the Garter, Her Majesty the Queen can alone bestow. This carving shows the Scottish crown with Scotland's national flower, the tough prickly thistle defending the surrounding chain. From it hangs the figure of Scotland's patron saint, Saint Andrew, nailed to the Saltire, the cruelest form of crucifixion, from whose slanting shape our country derives its national flag.

Next comes the Order of the Holy Roman Empire, whose territory occupied much of what is now the Republic of Germany. This award is known as the Order of the Golden Fleece, from the horned ram that hangs from it, indicating the wealth and importance of the woolen industry to this part of Europe. Notice also the castellated keeps and the heraldic lions.

Finally, on the right and very appropriately nearest to St Michael's church is the French Order of St Michael, with its golden *fleur de lys*, that country's national flower. This shield is a fitting reminder of the 'auld alliance' and the friendship that for over seven hundred years has formed a bond between Scotand and France. Today, it is brought to life in Linlithgow through the Burgh's twinning with Guyencourt, the new town near the former royal palace at Versailles to the south of Paris. Under the chairmanship of Ian Donaldson, the link between Linlithgow and Guyancourt celebrated its tenth anniversary in 1999. Activities have ranged from rugby matches to classical concerts, with ever-increasing involvement between the youth of the two towns. The scallop shells are a reminder of earlier continental travels when pilgrims used to carry them to ward off seasickness. After the Reformation they were looked upon as Papish relics, thus their mention in the verse, 'Mary, Mary, quite contrary, how does your garden grow, with cockleshells and silver bells and pretty maids all in a row.' Now sung as a nursery rhyme, it was originally a satire aimed at the Scottish Queen and her ladies-in-waiting due to their attendance at Mass, in which the ringing of the bells indicates the presence of the Host.

The Roman Catholic Church still has a strong presence and loyal congregation in Linlithgow. This picture postcard from the 1950s shows the shrine to the Virgin Mary in the grounds of St Michael's Roman Catholic Church. Linlithgow is unique amongst Scottish towns in having two places of worship sharing exactly the same name, both. designed by the distinguished architect Peter Paul Pugin, whose most famous building is the Palace of Westminster in London. When it was being built in the mid-1880s it was announced that it would be called the Queen Mary Memorial Chapel, but in 1887, Archbishop Smith of the Diocese of St Andrews and Edinburgh announced that the name of the Linlithgow parish would be changed from its original St Jospeh's, as the primary school is still known, to St Michael's, and from then on the fine new Gothic church bore this title. The shrine was erected by the soldiers of the Polish Army Ambulance Brigade who were stationed here during the Second World War. Behind are the buildings of Laetare, the international youth centre founded by Father Michael McGovern. The present priest is the Revd James Ferrari.

The Linlithgow Palace Junior Guides, founded by the author in 1978 to involve the young people of Linlithgow more closely in the history of their town and the active interpretation of it to visitors, wear the costumes of the reign of Mary Queen of Scots. Each year, approximately twenty pupils from the senior class at Linlithgow Primary School are trained to become guides, and here six of them are seen in front of the fountain.

A lot of restoration work has taken place at the palace as can be seen by its dilapidated state in this Victorian print. The famous triple-tiered fountain was in a particularly ruinous state. The fountain, with its figures representing the members of the Three Estates – the Lords, the Clergy and the Merchants – was added as an ornate finishing touch to the palace by King James V, when he gave it as a wedding present to his second wife, Mary of Guise. It was Sir Walter Scott, who paid Linlithgow Palace its finest tribute, when in his poem *Marmion* he wrote, 'Of all the palaces so fair, built for the royal dwelling, in Scotland far beyond compare, Linlithgow is excelling.'

This drawing shows the north façade of the courtyard as it was following its reconstruction. Notice the small windows beside the large ones. The bedrooms in this rebuilt block were among the first in the country to have their own individual facilities in the form of garderobes. The big drawback to this convenient arrangement was that, unfortunately, flushing water closets had yet to be invented. The result was that the use of the palace for royal visits had to be limited to two or three weeks in the summer or a month in winter. Thereafter, it had to be vacated so that the servants could undertake the unpleasant task known as 'the cleansing of the palace!'

This drawing of the south façade of the palace shows how it looked before the fire destroyed the roof and the elongated windows of the Chapel Royal in 1746, the New Entry having been constructed during the reign of King James V. The palace looks much less squat and much more in proportion with its sloping slate roof.

The imposing main east façade is depicted in this drawing showing the original main entrance which was reached by a drawbridge. High above the entrance the three angels guard the royal coat of arms. The view omits the four tall cap towers, originally there to guard this side of the palace and linked to it by flying butresses spanning the dry moat. The ruins of three of the towers can still be explored as seen in the photograph on page 58.

The courtyard of the palace was the setting for this 1960s Gala Day photograph. Amongst those posing with the Linlithgow and Linlithgow Bridge Gala Queen and her young retinue are from left to right: Councillor Margaret Glen, -?-, ex-Provost Sandy Merker, Mrs Merker, Mrs Daisy Marshall, Bailie Bob Marshall, Mrs Byrne, Provost Fergus Byrne, -?- , Bailie David Cook, Councillor Julia Wade, Burgh Surveyor Jim Flett, -?-, Mrs Bain and Councillor Peter Bain, mine host at the Red Lion Inn. Above them on the fountain are the stone-carved figures of the lieges of Linlithgow in the Middle Ages, including the town drummer, a merchant and the priest.

Bonnie Prince Charlie visited Linlithgow Palace on the morning of Sunday 15 September. Linlithgow's Jacobite supporters were led by Mrs Glen Gordon and it is said that this was the last occasion on which the fountain in the palace courtyard ever ran with red wine instead of water. Noticeable by his absence, however, was Provost John Buckney, who although he was known to have Jacobite sympathies, apparently felt that it was more discreet for a man in his position to stay out of sight and absented himself by riding off to Edinburgh. He could not, however, prevent his wife and daughters from attending the reception at which they delighted the prince in their tartan dresses. The Prince's visit to Linlithgow is re-enacted each summer as part of the series of short dramas presented by the Linlithgow Festival Trust.

The remains of the massive masonry fore towers which guarded the east façade of Linlithgow Palace are seen in this view of the original entrance. It was reached by a drawbridge that spanned the dry moat and led across to the grassy bank on the left. The hollow in the grass is known locally as the 'Giant's Cradle' and is a traditional place for Linlithgow children to keep up the old custom of rolling their colourfully decorated hard-boiled eggs every Easter. The old entrance is pointed out to tourists as the place where Farmer Binny rescued the palace from the English, but his heroic act actually took place over a century before the construction of the stone-built palace.

Finally in this section, we return to the foot of the Kirk Gate to see Cross House as it looked in the years when it was a bed and breakfast establishment. The improvements made to this eighteenth century building since it was taken over by St Michael's church can be appreciated by looking at this photograph. Even more renovations have taken place at the rear of Cross House, which was originally the yard belonging to local joiner John Brock. The fine church hall, which has been built on the site of the old lock up garages, has been designed by well-known local architect Thom Pollock, whose Pollock Hammond Practice specializes in the restoration of historic buildings from cottages to castles.

Five

The Riding of the Marches

Every year, on the first Tuesday after the second Thursday in June, Linlithgow relives its past when all the lieges are commanded to turn out for the annual Riding of the Marches. The day begins at dawn to the beat of the drum and the sound of the flutes. This early start was dictated by the necessity for the Burgh Treasurer to have time to bring all of his books up to date and ready for presentation at the Provost's Breakfast. This is still the first big set piece of the memorable day ahead. Originally, besides porridge with cream and bacon and eggs, salt herring were also always on the menu to ensure guests worked up a good 'drouth' for all of the toasts which lay ahead. While the Provost entertains his official guests, including the Deacons and their right-hand men from all of the organizations about to take part in the Riding, the organizations from the Dyers to the members of the Forty-One Club, and most recently the members of the Rotary Club of Linlithgow and Bo'ness, whose presence has replaced that of the original trade guilds, hold their own breakfasts. Well-dined, they then make their way to the forecourt in front of the palace for the fraternization, during which they shake hands with Provost, Bailies, Magistrates and Councillors. Together they then march down the Kirk Gate to the Cross for the Fencing of the Court, during which the official Town Crier reads the traditional proclamation. As the Town House clock chimes eleven o'clock, the procession led by the horse drawn carriages carrying the Provost and other dignitaries then moves off west along the High Street to inspect the first of the boundaries at Linlithgow Bridge. There, despite the 1998 ban on the consumption of alcholol outdoors in public places, toasts are still drunk from the Waldie Loving Cup, before the procession forms up again to ride all the way back through the town to Low Port and then on all the way to Blackness. This is an especially important part of the day's proceedings as Blackness was originally Linlithgow's seaport, through which much of its commerce was transacted. After a pause for the laying of wreaths at the war memorial in front of the church at the foot of the long steep hill leading down to the harbour, the participants proceed on foot down into the village, where they are refreshed with cooling glasses of Blackness Milk, a much more potent brew than the cows deliver on any other day of the year as it is liberally laced with whisky. The assembled crowd is then addressed by the Baron Bailie, who fills a time honoured office as, due to all of its three-mile distance from the Royal and Acient Burgh, Blackness was considered in need of its own magistrate. In the Middle Ages he had considerable powers to maintain law and order in the port, including the right to order the flogging of any sailors who refused to obey his commands. Today, his main duty is to deliver his annual report on Marches Day. After he has done so, the company then climbs Castle Hill for the ceremony of the Fencing of the Court near the ruins of St Ninian's Chapel overlooking the Castle. The Provost's party then returns to the village square where the old Guildry (the warehouse of the Linlithgow merchants) used to stand to enjoy lunch in a marquee specially erected for the occasion. Here, the Deacons and their Lords from all the other organizations present their loyal greetings before joining their own groups for lunch, whence in turn, the Provost dispatches his representatives to return the honour. At five o'clock all reassemble at Low Port for the final procession of the day along the crowd-packed High Street to ride the traditional lucky three times round the Cross, but not before hundreds more photographs have been taken. The small selection which follows tries to capture some of the flavour of Linlithgow's big day.

'Oyez, Oyez, Oyez. The burgesses, craftsmen and whole inhabitants of Linlithgow are hereby warned and summoned to attend my Lord Provost, Bailies and Council at the ringing of the bells on Tuesday for the purpose of riding the Town's Marches and liberties according to the use and custom of the ancient and honorable Burgh. And that in their best carriage, equipage, apparel and array also to attend all diets of the court held and appointed on that day by my Lord Provost and Bailies and that under the penalty of One Hundred Pounds Scotch each. God save the Queen and My Lord Provost', announces the official Town Crier at the Crying of the Marches which always takes place at lunchtime on the Friday before the big day. Traditionally the Crier is accompanied by the town halberdiers. On this occasion they were Crier Sandy Pagan and halberdiers and true Black Bitches David Morrison and Willie Renton. Equally by tradition, these town officials are also accompanied by a drummer and flute players, as well as by hordes of school bairns. From the fact that one wee laddie has stripped down to his semmit, it would appear that on this particular occasion the Crying took place on a scorching hot Friday, warranting well for the events of the following Tuesday.

At this Crying before the First World War, the crowd outside the Victoria Hall was so large that it completely blocked the High Street. The contrast in the dress of the children in this photograph from those in the previous picture is very marked, with the girls wearing straw sun hats and the boys their school caps, even on this hot day. Again the weather does appear to have been fine and warm. This card was one of a series published by the local chemist and newsagent, C.M. Spence.

Town Crier Tommy Cockburn bawls out his announcement, guarded by halberdiers Peter Hunter and George Fleming. On other days of the year, Mr Hunter was the town plumber and was widely known by his nickname, Cold Water Pete.

The final Crying traditionally took place beneath the branches of Katie Wearie's Tree at West Port as seen in this picturesque postcard from the early years of the 1900s, when the Town Crier was Sam Weir and the halberdiers were Bamberry and Harvey. 'Poodle' Bowie was the drummer and was accompanied by flautist Muir. By the 1980s road safety considerations dictated a move into the playground of Linlithgow Primary School's West Port Annexe. Such an official acceptance of the Crying by the school authorities would no doubt have amused former pupil David Morrison. As an exiled Black Bitch he wrote the following letter home. 'I see myself again as a Burgh School pupil longing for the Friday preceding the great event, when the Town Herald, Jock the Blackie, attired in his new velvet suit with red stockings and buckled shoes and cocked bonnet with feather, gathered us all around him for the Crying. Like a great orchestra leader he would direct and time us with his drumstick in the opening, 'Yez, O Yez,' 'Yez' of his proclamation. Again I am keeping in step to the 'Roke', played by flautist Muir and drummer Bowie as I find myself marching along the High Street with my schoolmates. I leave the crowd at the Cross and return to the Burgh School, realizing that if I were late, 'Baldie' or 'Bull Dog' Walker, or 'Coal Jack' Forrester would greet me with tawse!' Now Linlithgow pupils need not hurry back to classes as every Friday afternoon is a holiday thanks to West Lothian Council's asymmetric school week. The threat of the strap was abolished on 1 April 1981.

Town Crier Collins and his accompanying halberdiers took a break from their Marches Day duties to pose for this photograph in front of the fountain in the palace courtyard. He is carrying the town's famous drum, which survived the Penisular War in Spain between Britain and France during Napoleonic times at the beginning of the 1800s. Linlithgow Town Council was sadly abolished in 1975 as the result of Lord Wheatley's ill conceived reform of local government in 1975, robbing Linlithgow of its independence to look after its own affairs. The historic drum also went missing temporarily when West Lothian County Council took over the running of the town, but thanks to the persistant efforts of former Provost Jim Shanks, it was safely returned. The drum is now proudly displayed as part of the Linlithgow Story at the Historic Trust's headquarters at Annet House.

Even the baby was carried out into the High Street for the Crying of the Marches in the year 1905. Notice the schoolboys' Eton collars and school caps and the girls' pinafore style dresses.

In 1932 the Kirk Gate was jam-packed with enthusiastic Marches supporters as they made their way down to the Cross following the Fraternization. Just beyond the arch of the Outer Yett can be spotted Provost Dougal and his Bailies and Magistrates in their ermine trimmed robes. The band is thought to be Kinneil Silver Band from Bo'ness. Notice the headgear of the spectators standing against the walls on either side of the road, with flat caps for the men folk and cloche hats for the ladies.

In 1930 after the Fencing of the Court at the Cross, the Gazette Trophy was presented for the first time to the clipped box wood covered horse-drawn float seen here making its way along the High Street with the towers and turrets of the Victoria Hall in the background. It was entered by J. McCabe of Porterside Farm and the presentation was made by Mr Fred Johnston, publisher of the *Linlithgowshire Journal and Gazette*. The first floor house on the right was the home of the manager of the British Linen Bank and his son Leslie T. Montgomery recorded a vivid impression of his view from it of the Marches in his young days. He wrote, ' On one day of the year the sham balconies that ran across the face of the building actually played the part for which they appeared intended. On Marches Day there is a steady build up of excitement from early morning and I spend most of the day perched outside until by teatime the pace quickens and events reach their triumphant climax. As soon as a lookout on top of the Council Buildings sees the head of the procession returning from the east, the bells go mad. The returning procession circles the Cross once, then the leading horse-drawn carriages do it again and yet again at an ever quickening pace. Finally, the leading coaches arrive at a gallop in front of the Council Chambers. The year I remember most was when one of the lead horses of the four pulling the Provost's carriage went down with a snapping of shafts. As luck would have it that year the Provost was a master saddler. As quick as a flash he was out of the carriage, his ceremonial robes kilted up and the horse's head firmly sat on to prevent it struggling and impaling itself on the broken shaft.'

Four years earlier in 1928, well-known local character Baldie and one of his friends managed to acquire horses from Harry Shields the butcher, whose premises were to the east of the Clydesdale Bank where the hairdresser's premises are now situated, for the Riding. They are pictured as they rode past the hairdressers and tobacconists who occupied the shop adjacent to the Victoria Hall. Baldie was dressed as the Terrible Turk, a joke apparently at the expense of the then Rector of Linlithgow Academy, Mr Beveridge, who was nicknamed 'The Old Turk.

The start of a 1930s Marches procession. By tradition the town's bells are supposed to ring out from this moment until it passes the Horse Market Head beyond the West Port, before passing out of sight as it continues on west to Linlithgow Bridge. Earlier Marches used to feature the distinctive banners and floats of each of the trade guilds. The guild members loved to decorate their float to represent their own craft, often with examples of the goods which they produced. The Hammermen, who worked with metal, therefore decorated their float with an anvil and a large hammer, while the Guild of Wrights , who were the joiners and cabinet makers, decorated their pony-drawn trap with curly wood shavings and carried a small work bench at which the cut out figures of two joiners sawed away, their arms powered by elastic bands, and each pulled in turn by the youngest apprentice. The craft guild floats also boasted slogans. The Cordiners, who were the leather workers, proudly proclaimed, 'Our trade is ever lasting' and 'True to the last', while the Baxters asked, 'Can man live by bread alone?' with the snappy answer, 'Yes, if its baked by Oliphants!' The Dyers' motto is, 'We live to die, we dye to live.'

Although, unlike the Border 'riding of the marches' ceremonies, Linlithgow has never sported a 'braw lad' and his mounted followers, horses have, nonetheless ,always played an important part in the procession, as seen in this postcard photograph of a 1920s or early 1930s event.

C.M. Spence photographed the members of the Whipmen's Fraternity in the High Street to the east of the Cross outside what was then Hutton's Boot and Shoe Warehouse. The piper is the legendary Piper Dumbreck, and the drumer is Poodle Bowie. Unlike membership of one of the town's trade guilds, membership of a fraternity did not imply any actual link with the job described. Linlithgow orginally had eight societies of incorporated trades and six fraternities or friendly societies, each led by their respective Deacons. The eight guilds, in the order that they are earliest recorded as riding the Marches in 1687, are the Hammermen, the Tailors, the Baxters, the Cordiners, the Weavers, the Wrights, the Coopers and the Fleshers. The fraternities were the Gardiners, the Tanners, the Whipmen, the Skinners, the Curriers and the Dyers, of whom only the last still takes an active part in the Marches. The role of the fraternities was to provide welfare benefits, such as sickness pay, widows' pensions and even burial payments for their members and their families. Each fraternity had its treasurer or 'box master' as he was always known, because originally all of the funds were kept in a large, locked wooden or metal kist.

Crowds turned out in force to watch as the members of the Dyers, in their familiar uniform of formal black morning suits and grey toppers, made the traditional three rounds of the Cross at the end of the Marches celebrations in 1991. (Picture by kind permission of Thom Pollock)

Earlier on Marches morning the members of Linlithgow Reed Band lined the sides of the Kirk Gate as the Town Crier, who is dispatched from the Provost's Breakfast in the Burgh Halls, led the Dyers to the Fraternization in the palace forecourt. The photographers captured the scene from their vantage point atop the wall surrounding St Michael's Kirkyard. (Picture by kind permission of Thom Pollock)

This fine pair of greys pulled Provost Jim White's open landau at the 1993 Marches. The halberdier on the front carriage is Tom Grant and on the second carriage, David Jamieson. The carriage is seen passing the flats at the West Port end of the High Street. The much-criticized appearance of these blocks of four-storey high flats has been improved at least slightly by the addition of raked slated roofs. (Picture by kind permission of Thom Pollock)

On the way back from the town's western boundary at Linlithgow Bridge, on that same Marches Day in 1993, Provost White chose to lead his official party on foot past West Port House, Linlithgow's oldest occupied house, and past the starkly modern four-storey flats on the opposite side of the High Street. Over six years later this block of flats still sticks out like a very sore thumb on the Linlithgow landscape as West Lothian Council has failed to take the promised remedial action. (Picture by kind permission of Thom Pollock)

Provost White, with his Bailies and Magistrates in their ermine-trimmed robes, leads his guests past the West Port flats, from whose balconies householders and friends look down on the colourful scene. (Picture by kind permission of Thom Pollock)

Provost White's official guests at the 1993 Marches. From left to right, West Lothian Convener Councillor Jimmy McGinley, well-known local architect Thom Pollock and the Lord Lyon King at Arms' Herald, Charles Burnett, smile from their open horse-drawn landau as it passes the Cross and the frontage of the dress shop operated for many years by Marlyn Morris. (Picture by Clare Pollock)

Provost Sandy Merker and his guests enjoy sunshine as they drive along the High Street in an open landau.

A pair of greys drew this early horse-drawn bus. Its passengers included Burgh Surveyor Mr James Flett, Councillor John Geddes, Councillor Mel Gray and popular local GP Dr David Reid.

A carriage filled with provosts from surrounding Burghs was photographed as it passed Crawford Lamb the chemists. Over the archway of the pend can be made out the words 'Alex Hardie and Sons, Tanners and Curriers', indicating the entrance to that well- known leather making firm's premises on the lochside.

Another of Linlithgow's best-known firms was William Aitken of Stockbridge, from whose fleet of lorries came this impressive steam traction engine whose decorations won it first prize at the Marches in 1925. The gentlemen who posed in front of it for the photographer were all decked out in their Sunday best suits for the big day.

This Aitken entry for a Marches competition was photographed outside the firm's Stockbridge headquarters. Aitken's premises stood on the site which became Appleyards Garage and filling station and is now occupied by the BP filling station.

A great deal of work went into decorating Aitken's annual entry for the Marches procession and the lorry often made the round of other local festivities from Bo'ness Fair to Armadale Gala. In this day of automatic chokes, it is interesting to notice the manual starting handle on the front of the vehicle below the radiator. The driver had to take great care when using a starting handle as it often kicked back and could cause a painful injury to his leg.

Hands in jacket pockets, these school boys in their grey flannel shorts stroll beside this rival to Aitkens in the Marches parade. It was entered by Nobel's Explosives Company and was crowded with Marches revellers, but it may not have been the most comfortable of rides as the white painted tyres were of the solid variety. This was the first occasion on which female employees from the explosives works rode the Marches.

These delighted young men, including John Smith and John Orr, posed with their prize winning float outside the bank building in the High Streets in the days when it was still the National Commercial Bank of Scotland Ltd. Their very neatly finsihed Viking longship entry for the Marches procession was decorated with colourful crepe paper flowers, which were usually produced by the score by mothers, wives and girlfriends.

Derek Pattle provided the rearguard as this crowded float left the Cross for the trip out to Linlithgow Bridge at the 1991 Marches. The trailer was specially designed and built by well-known local agricultural equipment dealer and devoted Marches supporter John Kerr of Wilcoxholm Farm, whose trailers are also a popular attraction with members of the public at every summer's annual Royal Highland Show at Edinburgh's Ingliston Show Ground. (Picture by kind permission of Thom Pollock)

The fencing of the Court in 1938 took place, as was the custom in pre-Second World War years, in the High Street outside the famous Hole 'In the Wa' pub. This is believed to have been the first time that the Town Crier used a microphone to read his traditional proclamation and to make his announcements. Those in the picture include Provost John Mackay, Bailie Alex Ford, Bailie J. Russell Fleming, who was church organist at St Michael's and a well-known music teacher in the town, Bailie Bennie, Town Crier Bob Ireland, Town Clerk Norman Main, a well-known local weather expert Mr Gray, Councillor James Borthwick and Mr Morrison.

A very young looking Tam Dalyell of the Binns joined the visiting provosts from surrounding towns on the occasion of this Marches Procession in the early 1960s. Tam has represented first the Parliamentary Constituency of West Lothian and now the Linlithgow seat for almost forty years. This picture may have been taken on the occasion of the first Marches after his first election as Labour MP. (Picture by kind permission of the *Linlithgowshire Journal and Gazette*)

Toasts at the Brig, in the years when the Bridge Inn belonged to the well-known Batitisons. Provost Dougal is seen offering the Waldie Loving Cup to one of the Deacons of the Dyers, Bailie Peter Baird. Also in the picture is long serving Baron Bailie, Willie Spence.

This very inventive entry from the West Lothian Scout Association transformed the boys into dusky South Sea maidens as they canoed their way through the town. The white pith helmets are a reminder that many Linlithgow families had such headpieces in their attics due to younger members seeking fame and fortune in the lands of the British Empire in Africa and Asia.

'The Wee Yins', the sons and daughters of Linlithgow Bridge's well known 'Young Yins,' provided this very imagininative circus clown float at the 1996 Marches. Enthusiasm for the Marches is encouragingly buoyant amongst Linlithgow's Black Bitch whelps, and it is good to know that they will ensure the old traditions are loyally maintained long into the Millenium. (Picture by kind permission of Thom Pollock)

This Fire Brigade Deacon entered fully into the spirit of the occasion at the installation ceremony carried out on the two Saturday nights prior to the Marches. Old County Buildings, completed as West Lothian County Council's seat of local administration in 1939 can be seen in the background. It stands on the site formerly occupied by the old drill hall, so called because it was where the local volunteers used to practice their army exercises in Victorian times.

The photographer who snapped the following shots in black and white is unknown, but has done such an excellent job of capturing the atmosphere of a recent Marches Procession that I feel they should be included to bring the story of the big day up to date. This first picture captures the sizeable number of the crowd who joined in by marching with the procession as it climbed the brae at Stockbridge and passed Highfield Housing Estate on its return from the Brig.

From babies in push chairs to toddlers and young parents, this picture sums up the enthusiasm which still exists for the Marches amongst the younger generation of Black Bitches.

'Long Live The Marches' reads the slogan on this little tractor-pulled float and expresses the local sentiment for the big day.

An accordion band added to the fun of this Marches Day procession as Deacon Norman Cummings and his wife Joy pushed baby daughter Jacqueline up the brae at Stockbridge.

Majorettes in their colourful costumes have been another popular addition to recent Marches Day processions.

This armoured personnel vehicle added a rather bizarre note to this Marches procession.

That same year's procession did however still feature horses, including this fine pair of Clydesdales pulling the Buchanan's Black and White Whisky float. One army officer appears to have hitched a lift!

There were also horse-drawn floats heading for Low Port in this earlier Marches procession, pictured at the opposite end of the town as it passed the long stone wall which surrounded the old Nobles and later ICI's Regent Works. The works site is now occupied by the Regent Shopping Centre. When the foundation stone of the shopping centre was laid, the occasion was marked by the burial of a time capsule. It is from Low Port that the Marches procession makes its way out into the countryside, past Champany, said to take its name from the days when Mary Queen of Scots and her French courtiers enjoyed their picnics *á la campagne*, and on down to Blackness, which is described in the next section.

Six

Linlithgow's Little Port

Looking at the shore at Blackness nowadays, it is difficult to believe that in medieval times this was the second busiest port in Scotland, whose trade was exceeded only by Edinburgh's port of Leith. During these centuries Scotland's roads were underdeveloped and in a very poor state of repair. In winter what roads existed were muddy quagmires, while in summer they were deeply rutted dust bowls, which made their negotiation by any kind of wheeled vehicle practically impossible. The only way to transport cargo was therefore by ship, and great importance was attached to Scotland's seaports, especially to Leith and Blackness, vital to the supply of provisions for the royal courts at Holyrood and Linlithgow. Up until the sixteenth century, sailing ships were small, and while Blackness did have a short stone pier, vessels were usually simply beached on the shore for unloading. The first threat to the importance of Blackness as a port came in 1601, when its near neighbour Borrowstounness, three miles further up river, first began trading unoffcially as a port. Linlithgow immediately protested about Bo'ness, as it became known for short, and demanded that its harbour be closed because of the damage that it was doing to its port at Blackness. Linlithgow also strengthened its case by detailing the amount of smuggling which was allegedly taking place through the new upstart harbour. For a time the authorities did order the closure of Bo'ness, but as it was a better harbour, ships soon began to load and unload at it again. By this time Blackness had suffered a second blow as the removal of the Scottish Royal Court to Scotland Yard in London after the Union of the Crowns meant a disastrous decline in trade in connection with Linlithgow Palace. The importance of Blackness Castle also declined. By the end of the seventeenth century, however, Blackness was still of sufficient importance to be the provisioning port for several of the ships of the Darien Expedition before they departed on their ill-fated voyage to Central America. The Darien scheme was a disastrous attempt by the Scots to try to gain entry to the lucrative colonial trade, which until then England had kept as its closed shop. Its costly failure did, however, result in the Union of the Parliaments in 1707, and this meant that Scotland was henceforth included under the terms of the Navigation Acts. These acts declared that all commerce between Britain and her colonies had to be conducted by ships of the colony of origin or by British ships and that all goods had to be landed in this country, no matter where their eventual destination. The latter clause led to the growth of the Scottish tobacco industry. This involved the import of tobacco through Port Glasgow on the Clyde and its transport across the narrow waist of Scotland in horseback panniers to be re-exported from the East Coast to the Low Countries, where it was manufactured into high-quality cigars. As Blackness was the easiest port to reach, its trade boomed. The most famous name connected with the tobacco trade in Blackness and Linlithgow was that of the Mitchells. Their Prize Crop became so successful that they were able to donate some of their profits to provide Glasgow with its Mitchell Library. The tobacco trade came to a sudden halt in 1776 when the rebellion of the American colonies made the terms of the Navigation Acts irrelevant . Like all British East Coast ports, Blackness suffered during the long drawn out Napoleonic War. By the time it ended in 1815, the rise in importance of the United States and the resultant Atlantic trade meant the further enhancement of ports on the West Coasts and the continued decline of small East Coast harbours like Blackness. In Victorian times, however, Blackness found a new trade when a pier was built at the castle and it became the Central Ammunitions Depot for Scotland, thus avoiding the danger of transporting such dangerous materials overland. Blackness was garrisoned until the end of the First World War and the Scottish Baronial officers' quarters and much plainer barracks for the soldiers can be seen beside the historic castle, where the pier used to land the explosives has also recently been restored.

Blackness, Linlithgow's port, takes its name from the 'nez' or nose of black basalt igneous rock on the tip of which its formidable castle dominates the south side of the River Forth, as this picture shows clearly.

Blackness is often known as Scotland's Ship Shape Castle, and this picture shows the Stern Tower on the landward side, the tall Main Mast Tower amid ships and the Fore Castle or Fo'scle Tower jutting straight out into the river. The experts at Historic Scotland insist unimaginatively that Blackness acquired the appearance of a medieval stone sided man 'o war, simply because of its geographic location, but local tradition insists that there is a much more colourful story to relate about its ship like shape. According to it, Blackness became Scotland's ship shape castle because the country's Lord High Admiral of the Fleet, Admiral Douglas, during the reign of King James V, was plagued with seasickness. Desperate at all costs to avoid going to sea, Douglas is said to have promised King Jamie that he would provide Scotland's navy with 'a ship that the English could never sink.' Blackness was the result, and in true Gilbert and Sulivan fashion, Blackness Castle became the admiral's landbased headquarters! The Provost of Linlithgow is still the Vice Admiral of the Forth, and during his term of office Provost Hector Woodhouse invited the Admiral, Lord Provost of Edinburgh Sir Norman Irons, to join him at a Marches ceremony.

82

During the peaceful Norman Conquest of Scotland in the twelfth century, the lands upon which Blackness Castle stands came into the possession of the De Viponts of Carriden, and they may have built a fortified tower to defend their estate. The buildings seen today date from the 1440s when they were erected by Sir George Crichton, brother of the Chancellor of Scotland. He gifted it to King James II in 1453 and the castle has since then always belonged to the crown.

In 1537 work began to strengthen the Stern Tower. It was completed by 1543, by which time it had lived up to its description well as 'a great brute mass of masonry.' Blackness held out in support of Mary Queen of Scots from her abdication in 1567 until 1573. During this time, despite a government blockade, its French garrison managed to cause damage to shipping in the Forth, until finally tricked into surrender. The castle then became Scotland's version of Château d'If, as it became a grim state prison, mainly for religious prisoners. It last saw action in the 1650s when it was besieged by Oliver Cromwell's army, and bombarded from both land and sea with the Devil having been reported to have appeared during one of the explosions!

The De'il is also claimed to have been a frequent visitor to the House of Binns, the ancestral home of the Dalyell family, which stands on the hillside above Blackness overlooking the castle and is reputedly linked to it by a secret underground tunnel. The name Dalyell is, of course, pronounced the same as De'il, and Auld Nick is indeed said to have been entertained at the historic house by the much hated General Tam Dalyell, an ancestor of the present Labour Member of Parliament of the same name, who occupies the house as his family has always done since the Binns was first built in 1612. The unusual name of the house is derived from the Gaelic word 'ben', meaning a hill, and well describes its lofty position above the village and the castle. The Binns was the scene of the raising of the Royal Scots Greys in 1681, the only British regiment ever founded with a royal title from the time of its origin.

This striking oil painting of 'Bloody Tam' as the Covenanters nicknamed General Dalyell, founder of the Royal Scots Greys, hangs in Old County Buildings in Linlithgow's High Street. It shows him clean shaven, but as a supporter of the royal House of Stuart he vowed not to cut his hair or beard from the time of the execution of King Charles I in 1649 until the restoration of the monarchy with Charles II in 1660. It was during his campaign in support of the king against the Covenanters that he is claimed to have entertained the Devil at the Binns. It appears to have been a tempestuous relationship, so much so that the De'il threatened to blow the house down and Dalyel retaliated by building the turreted towers seen in the previous picture. On another occasion when the Devil lost at gaming, it is alleged that he threw the marble-topped card table out of the house and true enough it was later retrieved from the pond in the grounds. The Binns is claimed to be Scotland's most haunted home and the pond is home to a gleaming black water kelpie while the grounds are home to a ghostly brown-clad Pict. General Tam himself often joins the ghostly clan riding home at midnight on his grey battle charger.

Following the First World War, Blackness was predicted to become a major Scottish tourist resort. A few holiday homes were built and hopes were greatly boosted in the 1930s, when this composite picture postcard was printed, as Blackness Bay was tipped to become the major passenger seaplane base for the East of Scotland. Again, however, hopes were dashed by the ending of passenger seaplane services by the outbreak of the Second World War in 1939. Peace in 1945 brought another burst of hope that Blackness would develop into a top seaside place, when the village was inspected by officials from the Butlins holiday organization, but Sir Billy decided instead to build his Scottish camp on the other side of the country at Heads of Ayr. The central view on this card shows the unusually designed village church with its central spire and, in front of it, the village war memorial. While men from the area gave their lives in both world wars, Blackness itself has remained a delightfully peaceful little place.

This is another picture postcard view of Blackness, this time in the Spence's Linlithgow Series. Looking from the west it shows the old Guildry after it was converted from being a warehouse, belonging as the name indicates to the Guilds of Linlithgow, into a tenement of houses. The historic, massive thick stone-walled Guildry was unfortunately demolished during the 1960s in an act of official local authority council vandalism. Even more unfortunately, instead of at least leaving a clear view from the village square out over the river, West Lothian County Council then replaced it with a hideous block of modern flats, which to this day remains a blot on the village seascape. This picture was taken from the upstairs window of Low Valleyfield House, which is still the home of descendants of the well-known Spence family. On Marches Day the marquee for the provost's party to take lunch is now erected on the former tennis court at Low Valleyfield.

Again from Spence's Linlithgow Series, this early picture postcard view taken form the west from the window in the opposite gable wall of Low Valleyfield House, shows how much more crowded the village of Blackness was at the start of the twentieth century. The original three-storeyed facade of the Blackness Inn is seen on the extreme right, with the village shop, post office, tearoom and hall visible on the far side of the Square. Notice that the shop is still a one-storeyed building, in contrast to how it appears in the picture at the top of page 85.

The original Blackness Inn, village store, post office and hall are all seen to advantage in this early twentieth century picture postcard view taken from the north side of the Square. A modern two-storey version of the inn still flourishes and is a very pleasant place to both eat and drink down by the waterside. Sadly, the shop, post office, tearoom and hall have all closed and have now been transformed into private houses. Before its closure the tearoom was transformed into the Hamlet Restaurant, a reminder that Blackness enjoyed tremendous publicity when the castle was chosen for film producer Franco Zifferelli's version of the Shakespeare epic *Hamlet* featuring Australian film star Mel Gibson. As well as providing a setting for the Danish tragedy, Blackness has also enjoyed large and small screen fame in *The Bruce*, starring Sean Connery's son, Jason, and in the BBC television version of Sir Walter Scott's *Ivanhoe*. It is interesting to note the old black iron communal water pump. It still exists but has been moved to another site on the west side of the Square.

As a picturesque little seaside spot, Blackness has been well represented in postcard views and this one shows the village photographed from the east, and showing its distinctly rural nature. The wooden eaved building at the top of the grassy slope was at one time used as the village school, until it moved to Mannerstoun. It later became the village library and is now a private home.

This delightfully charming picture postcard view shows Blackness looking shoreward form the village pier. The white washed building to the right was the village byre, whose cows on Marches Day always succeeded in producing the potent whisky laced Blackness milk. The large attractive house in the centre of the picture, known as the Dairy, is now one of several homes in the area offering visitors bed and breakfast with the bonus of wonderful views across the River Forth.

Dinghies belonging to members of the Blackness Boating Club await the tide on the foreshore to the west of the castle. The boating enthusiasts delight in teasing visitors by telling them they are from the BBC. (Picture by kind permission of Ian Torrance)

From modern boats to an historic ship, or rather the beautifully made model of one that hangs in Blackness village church. This is *The Knowe*, so called because this intricately detailed model of a thirty-two gun fully rigged black frigate was discovered hidden in the attic of the house of that name, which stands on a hillside in the port of Bo'ness overlooking the Forth. This intirguing find was made by local joiners Archie and Jimmy Cuthell in 1965. Both enthusiastic sailors on the Forth and loyal members of Carriden parish church, whose sailors' aisle was already graced by a model of the *Ranger*, the brothers decided to donate *The Knowe* to Blackness Church. This means that all mariners entering its doors may know that they are formally welcomed to the church and are immediately reminded of the sea. After thirty years swinging at anchor in Blackness church, *The Knowe* was dry docked in 1995 and given a complete overhaul by a Bo'ness model ship builder and tall ship enthusiast, Charlie Sneddon. During the painstaking refit, Mr. Sneddon carefully inspected all 2,000 pieces of *The Knowe's* rigging and was particularly intrigued to discover that the tiny necklace round the neck of the ship's little figurehead on the prow is made of real gold. *The Knowe* was formally rededicated on 7 April 1995. Her original builder, who lavished such care on this magnificent model, will probably never be known. He can surely rest in the knowledge, however, that his vessel is much admired every Sunday by the congregation when the minister from Carriden parish church travels to the village to lead them in worship at Blackness church. (Picture by kind permission of Charlie Sneddon)

Seven

Barging Into Town

While throughout the middle ages Linlithgow's merchants had to travel to and from Blackness to import and export their goods, in 1822 the town acquired its own inland port with the completion of the Union Canal. Situated at Manse Basin, it soon became a hive of industry. The Union Canal, linking Edinburgh with Falkirk, where it connected with the already existing Forth and Clyde Canal to Glasgow and the West Coast, was one of the last canals to be built in Britain. As such it benefitted from all of the knowledge gained from earlier experiments in canal design. Time wasting locks were avoided by constructing the whole of the canal's course at exactly the same level above sea level by following the 240 feet contour line for its entire thirty-one miles. Indeed, the Union Canal was planned so precisely by its architect and engineer John Baird that it was nicknamed the Mathematical River as it maintained a constant depth of five feet and a constant width of thirty-five feet. It was constructed mainly to transport heavy cargoes of stone to build Edinburgh's blocks of tenements and later equally heavy cargoes of coal with which to fuel 'Auld Reekie's' smoking chimneys, but was also used for a much swifter, streamlined, sixty-five foot long passenger barges. These barges provided a quicker and much more comfortable alternative to travelling between Edinburgh and Glasgow by bumpy stagecoach. The journey by express barge reduced the time taken between the two cities from twelve hours to only eight, a speed ensured by changing the teams of horses every eight miles at stables, some of which, like those at Woodcockdale and Kingscavil, are still landmarks along the length of the canal towing path. Wing path follows its north bank for its entire length and today forms a splendid linear park. Not only was the journey smoother by barge, it also offered the luxuries of dining and drinking aboard while some of the vessels even had their own libraries and dance floors with bands to provide the music for the more energetic passengers. Alternatively, passengers could choose to sleep their way across Scotland with a night express barge leaving Port Hopetoun in Edinburgh and port Dundas in Glasgow every night at 10 p.m. and arriving in the other city the following morning in ample time to do business. Due to the large lamps that they carried in their bows to light the course on their overnight journeys, the night express barges were nicknamed the 'Wee Hoolets' or the 'Little Owls', and they also became fashionable with honeymooners. Perhaps adding to the excitement of these overnight journeys may have been the knowledge that two of the labourers who had worked on the digging of the canal were none other than the most famous of the body snatchers, the resurrectionists or corpse vandals, Burke and Hare. The labourers who did the arduous task of excavating the canal were known as navvies, the name being derived from the fact that they navigated the course of the canal across the countryside. They were such a rough, tough crew that the people of Linlithgow demanded that the palace should be garrisoned with soldiers to protect them when the canal labourers celebrated pay night by getting drunk in the local inns.. This was the last time that troops were ever based at Linlithgow Palace. Even when the canal was completed, not all of the local people were happy, particularly the farmers around the town who feared that it might flood their fields. In the end, though, the farmers' crops benefited from the rich cargoes of ripe horse manure gathered from Edinburgh's city streets, which the empty stone and coal barges transported on their return voyages!

All dressed up in their best white frocks and smartest suits, these excited girls and boys crowded aboard this horse-drawn barge to sail from Manse Basin to Vellore and Caribber Glen for their annual summer Sunday school outing. The wisp of smoke rose from the stove in the boatman's cabin in the stern. In the background can be seen the old canal stables, which the enthusiasts of LUCS, the Linlithgow Union Canal Society, such as former councillor Mel Gray and his wife Dr Judy Gray, Deacon Barbara Braithwaite and former banker Colin Galloway, have converted into Scotland's only canal museum and tearoom. (Picture from the LUCS archive, taken by W. Allan Brown and loaned by his son Robert A. Brown)

Opposite: Human passengers in years gone by could apparently be a lot more troublesome than the wildlife on the canal, as this notice published in May 1844 indicates. By then the days of the barges being so crowded that some of the steerage or second-class passengers travelling in the stern might have to sit or stand outside were fast drawing to a close. The newfangled railway between Edinburgh and Glasgow with its station at Linlithgow was already robbing the barges of their trade. (Poster from the LUCS collection)

This barge of a century ago was pictured sailing past Jimmy Newton's coalyard at the top of Station Brae. The tradition of cruising on the canal is maintained every Saturday and Sunday afternoon from Easter to October by the flagship of the LUCS's fleet, *Saint Magdalene*, as she operates her ever-popular cruises to the Avon Aqueduct and the Slammanan Basin on the Falkirk side. The sleekly streamlined *Saint Magdalene* can carry forty passengers and is Scotland's only environmentally friendly all-electric barge. Her smooth, silent progress allows passengers close up views of the canal's rich and varied wildlife as the swans, ducks, coots and moorhens are completely undisturbed by her passage. For those with less time to spare, shorter half-hour cruises are also provided by the replica Victorian steam packet *Victoria*. (Picture from the LUCS collection)

NOTICE.

NO SMOKING allowed in any of the Union Canal Company's Passenger Boats.

No Person under the influence of Liquor shall be received on Board. If it shall be discovered that there is on Board any such Person, or any Person riotous or using improper Language, or who annoys others, such Person shall be put on Shore at the First Stables.

Passengers are requested not to reach over the Windows or Sides of the Boat, as doing so puts the Boat out of proper sailing trim.

No Person permitted to sit or stand outside the Steerage if there be room inside.

Canal Office, Edinburgh, May 1844.

This early picture postcard view shows the canal looking east towards Manse Basin. The tranquil scene was described by Victorian writer Alexander Smith, when he wrote in his essay *Dreamthorp*, 'Every now and then a horse comes staggering along the towing path, trailing a sleepy barge filled with merchandise. A quiet indolent life these bargemen lead in the summer days. One lies stretched at his length on the sun-heated plank, his companion sits smoking in the little dog-hutch which I suppose he calls a cabin. Silently, they come and go and silently the wooden bridge lifts to let them through. The horse stops at the bridge-house for a drink and there I like to talk a little with the men they serve instead of a newspaper, and retell with great willingness the news they have picked up in their progress from town to town.' The two-storey building still stands, but the little white cottage in the far distance has been demolished. It was the home of Davie Dodds, the town's road sweeper or the 'scavy' as he was always known, a name derived from the word scavenger. Davie always carried out his duties with great dignity, often wearing a tailcoat and black top hat. On one occasion he stood as a candidate for Linlithgow Town Council and polled eleven votes. At the announcement of the result of the ballot on the steps of the Town House, he proudly told the assembled crowd, 'Weel at least I ken noo that there's eleven folk in Linlithgow who are as daft as me!'

The replica Victorian steam packet *Victoria* was the first passenger vessel introduced by LUCS when it was launched in the mid-1970s. The smartly painted *Victoria*, which is still a great favourite with passengers on the canal, is seen here with Manse Road Bridge in the background.

Using the proverbial 'barge pole' to nudge *Victoria* away from the towing path on the north bank of the canal.

Imagining what it was like to be a canal horse pulling a heavy barge, young Rebecca Helliwell led the line on this Linlithgow Primary School project outing with her father John bringing up the rear. The Union Canal is a wonderful source of industrial archaeology and the pupils were filmed on this occasion for the Scottish Television series *History at Hand*. (Picture by kind permission of Jean Meldrum)

Adding to the spirit of this canal project, teacher Mrs Carol Jamieson and her pupils got all dressed up as bargees and navvies. (Picture by kind permission of Jean Meldrum)

Just give me the facts, man! Pupils from Linlithgow Primary School with clip boards at the ready, visited the Linlithgow Union Canal Society's museum at Manse Basin, where former rector of Linlithgow Academy John Ferguson organizes school day visits. (Picture by kind permission of Jean Meldrum)

The Union Canal is also an excellent place to enjoy nature study. At one period in the 1960s when the canal was a derelict rubbish filled ditch, parents campaigned to have it filled in. Now it is a much valued local asset and the Scottish Inland Waterways Association's slogan, 'A used canal is a safe canal', has been seen to be correct, with Linlithgow children now proving that they can be trusted to live and play safely along its banks. (Picture by kind permission of Jean Meldrum)

Part of the problem when the Union Canal was in a dreadfully derelict condition in the 1960s was that its water was culverted at Preston Road. Now the canal flows freely again thanks to the construction of this splendid new canal bridge, faced with stone from Huddersfield in Yorkshire, as none suitable could be found in Scotland. Early in the new Millenium, thanks to Lottery funding, all similar blockages on both the Union and Forth and Clyde Canals will be removed, including major obstructions at the M8 motorway, and it will once again be possible to sail right across Central Scotland. (Picture by Jean Meldrum)

As well as people, the swans are also enjoying the new found freedom of the restored Union Canal. The canal banks have never been sprayed with insecticides and therefore the trees, reeds and wild flowers all flourish along its towing path. To safeguard the swans from passing motorists the pupils from Linlithgow Primary School, whose Preston Road premises adjoin the canal, campaigned and persuaded the local West Lothian Roads Department to erect Scotland's first swan warning sign.

Another former vessel of the LUCS fleet, the *Janet Telford*, was built by engineering apprentices at Edinburgh's Telford College of Further Education. The Janet Telford also sailed on the River Clyde at the Glasgow Garden Festival and now plies on the Forth and Clyde Canal where she provides cruises for the handicapped operated by the Seagull Trust. Similar cruises backed by the Order of St John of Jerusalem are also operated on the Union Canal by the Seagull Trust from its bases at Ratho and Falkirk.

Eight
Linlithgow at Work and Play

In the past Linlithgow was a small market town, whose industries were also mainly connected with agriculture. Most famously the town was second only to Perth for the manufacture of leather, and tanneries lined the shores of the loch whose water was important in the manfacturing process. The fleshers who butchered the animals and the cordainers whose skill turned the hides into leather were always amongst the town's leading trade guilds. Nowadays Linlithgow's last tenuous link with the leather trade is through Morrisons shoe shop, in whose workshops the last of millions of pairs of Linlithgow-made shoes and boots were produced, but there is still work for fleshers at the local abbatoir, which the Henderson family have succeeded in turning into one of the largest and most efficient in Britain. Another well-known name connected with local industry is that of John G. Stein and Co. Ltd of Manuel, the world's top producer of refractory products such as high-temperature resistant Super Duty Fire Bricks for use in blast furnaces. These bricks contain over 43 per cent alumina, some of it mined on site. In addition, the factory manufactures special refractors using the highest quality alumina mixed with imported chrome and magnesite ores. All of its bricks are fired in huge 700ft-long gas- or oil-fired tunnels, which are the largest of their kind in the world. Founded in 1928, Stein and Co. Ltd. are a very important employer in the Linlithgow area, providing jobs for around 600 people.

Another well-known international industrial name who once had a factory in the town was Swedish manufacturer Alfred Nobel, who opened his Regent Works at Low Port in 1901 for the production of explosives. The thought of an explosives factory in the centre of Linlithgow would be unthinkable nowadays, but it was very much an accepted part of the life of the town for half a century, even after it switched production to produce ammunition during the First World War. The Nobel Works or the Explosives Factory as it became known, employed mainly women, many of whom travelled into the town each day from surrounding villages such as Avonbridge and Bridgend. It had a remarkably good safety record, but during the Second World War a major explosion killed either five or six women working in the incendiary department. Later Nobels changed to producing pharmaceutical products and was taken over by what was at the time Britain's largest company, Imperial Chemical Industries. ICI's later closure of the Regent Works was a severe blow to Linlithgow and the site is now occupied by the Regent Shopping Centre. The east end of Linlithgow was also the site of the town's famous St Magdalene's Distillery, whose distinctive buildings still survive, but which sadly is no longer in business. Nowadays the town's newest industries are American-owned Sun Micro, whose ultra modern purpose built computer plant occupies a large area at Burghmuir, and defence experts Racal, whose works are situated at Preston Road. There are also several enterprising smaller companies, such as industrial safety clothing manufactuer Arco, at the industrial estate at Linlithgow Bridge.

While Linlithgow has always been a town which has worked hard, it has also always had a reputation for playing hard. No matter whether Black Bitches choose to take their recreation on the rugby pitch or cricket field, the amateur drama stage or the dance floor, they set a high standard. While traditional sports such as greyhound racing at Mains Park, fox hunting in the Bathgate Hills, and point-to-point horse racing at Oatridge have fallen out of favour and disappeared, they have been replaced by modern sports ranging from squash and badminton to

Japanese martial arts. Another popular sport, which continues, but in a much altered fashion, is curling. It no longer involves a trip to the open air rink behind the Burgh Halls or waiting patiently for the ice on the loch to be declared 'bearing' for a bonspiel to beheld. The Linlithgow curlers now drive out of town to find the best artificial ice at various indoor rinks in Edinburgh, Stirling and other neighbouring towns, and in March 1999 those representing the local Rotary Club showed their prowess by winning the impressive Denny Kettle Trophy. Unlike the curlers, local golf enthusiasts are well catered for within and immediately around the town with two eighteen hole courses, one bordering the Union Canal and the other on top of the Erngath Hills with a popular driving practice range.

No summary of Linlithgow at play could be complete without mention of the town's favourite sons, the players of Linlithgow Rose Football Club. Linlithgow has been a football stronghold since the founding of the town's first team way back over a century ago in 1889. The earliest matches were played at Captain's Park at the east end of the town, and the team won its first major trophy at Tynecastle in 1902 when they defeated Inverkeithing Thistle in the Final of the Forth League Cup. In the 1920s all of the local county teams formed the West Lothian Junior league and the Rose won the first competition. In 1930 the Rose moved their headquarters to Mains Park and it was there the following year that their most famous signing Tommy Walker took the field at a cost to the club of three pounds and two shillings! After the Second World War, the Rose moved again to its present pitch at Prestonfield, which occupied the site of the old Gowan Stank Glue Works. Highlight of the Rose's career at Prestonfield came in 1965, when on 15 May at Hampden Park, Glasgow, before a 35,000 crowd they beat Baillieston Juniors 4-1 in the Final of the Scottish Junior Cup. That same season, apart form one competition, the Rose swept the board, adding to the Scottish Junior Cup, the Edinburgh District League Championship, the Brown Cup, the Lanark Lothian Cup and the East of Scotland Cup. The only trophy which escaped was the St Michael's Cup, and in that competition they reached the semi-final, only to lose 3-1 to Armadale Thistle. Ironically, it was Linlithgow lad Colin Stein who was mainly responsible for their defeat as he scored all of the goals in the Dale's win!

Linlithgow's earliest industries depended on waterpower from the River Avon with mills turning out products ranging from oatmeal and flour to silver. This early postcard view shows the big iron water wheel below the red pantiled roof at Little Mill.

The impressive railway viaduct carries the main Glasgow to Edinburgh railway line high over the valley of the River Avon as it enters the town from the west. The railway company dealt with Linlithgow in an equally high handed manner when the town tried to force it to pay tolls. In the end, being on the main line between the two cities has brought great benefits to Linlithgow as the convenience of rail travel has made it one of Scotland's fastest expanding commuter towns, but it took the Royal and Ancient Burgh many decades to appreciate this and to recover from its ill judged legal battle. (Picture by kind permission of John Doherty)

The arches of the railway viaduct tower over the fast flowing waters of the River Avon. (Picture by kind permission of John Doherty)

This cartoon of an emmaciated Black Bitch under the close scrutiny of a vulture perched on a branch of the town's shattered oak tree sums up the plight of Linlithgow when the town was bankrupted after it lost a Victorian court case. The town had been trying to levy a toll on every wagonload of goods which the new railway transported through the burgh similar to that which it had previously imposed on all road vehicles.

This early panoramic view of the town shows the railway station in the foreground with the huge water tank at the end of the platform to replenish the thirsty steam engines which hauled the trains. Equally interesting is the fact that it also shows on the left the thick stone-walled tower of the mint and in the centre, directly below St Michael's church, the historic premises of Linlithgow Burgh School. On the evening of 25 February 1902, the big open coal fire, which heated the school's large single classroom, could not have been put out properly when classes finished for the day and in the early hours of the morning the old school was gutted by fire. The town's volunteer firemen were called from their beds but there was little they could do when they rushed up the Kirk Gate as by then the water supply was frozen. By the time dawn broke, 'Auld Rusty Beard', as Rector Forbes was nicknamed by his pupils, found himself without a school. The delight of the boys and girls short lived, however, as they were soon merged with the pupils at the newly built Linlithgow Academy. The ruins of the old Grammar School were demolished.

This contemporary view, taken from the same position, shows how Linlithgow Railway Station has been modernized with a glass canopied waiting room on the south platform to provide shelter for those travelling west toFalkirk and Glasgow, and north to Stirling and Dunblane. In the background the Crown of Thorns provides an eye catching feature as it does to the thousands of passengers who pass through the town every day by train.

This picture, taken form Learmonth Gardens, shows another of Linlithgow's architectural curiousities, the beehive-shaped doo'cote. The thick stone-walled doo'cote is the only circular one in West Lothian. It is situated on what was originally the tail end of the long narrow runrig garden belonging to Baron Ross of Halkhead. It was home to over 800 pigeons, kept not for sport as in modern pigeon lofts, but for a welcome addition to the Halkhead family's food supply in the centuries when lack of winter fodder meant that all apart form breeding animals had to be slaughtered every autumn. Their meat was salted away for use during the coming months until fresh food became available again in the spring. Fresh pigeon meat, whether casseroled or baked, in what was known as a doo'cote pie, was therefore a most welcome winter delicacy, but it was only available to the nobles such as the Halkheads. The birds ate large quantities of grain, so keeping them was the privilege of the landed gentry. Such a valuable commodity had therefore to be safe guarded. Human predators were deterred by double locked iron doors, while animal predators, such as rats, were denied entry by the stone ropes or ridges that can be seen running round the building as they could not climb out and over them. The pigeon-holes through which the birds gained entry to the 400 nesting boxes that lined the interior from floor to ceiling can also be seen. There are other interesting doo'cotes of different designs in the attic of Hamiltons Land in the High Street and at Muiravonside Country Park. (Picture by kind permission of Ian Torrance)

The water of the River Avon had an important part to play in the production processes at the town's paper mills, which stood on its banks and whose tall chimneys are seen in this picture. The first of the two mills to open was Lochmill, already a growing concern when it was acquired in 1855 by Mr Thomas Chalmers. It occupied the site of a much earlier meal mill and Mr. Chalmers soon enlarged it. During the 1890s it became famous for the production of imitation art paper using imported esparto grass and the water finish process. Demand for this top quality paper was met by installing one of the largest paper making machines in the world with a net width of eighty eight inches, compared with the standard fifty five inches. Its top quality paper was used to produce the *Tatler* and *The Illustrated London News*. Always innovators, the Chalmers in more recent times used radio active isotopes to control the thickness of paper produced. The mill was subsequently purchased by the Inveresk Group, who sadly closed it as part of its reorganization of its paper-making interests. Lochmill's neighbour, Avonmill, operated by the Lovell family, specialized in making the finest quality writing paper until it closed in 1971. (Picture by kind permission of John Doherty)

The pagoda-style towers of St Magdalene's Distillery are still a landmark at the Low Port end of Linlithgow, although it is no longer in production. St Magdalene's was founded by Mr Sebastian Henderson and was famed for the malt whisky which it produced. It was at one time one of five distilleries in the town. St Magdalene's and its malt took their name from the hospital operated by the Knights of the Order of St John, who are reputed to have treated sufferers of leprosy.

Highlights of town's long and varied history are re-enacted on Sunday afternoons in the courtyard of the palace by members of the Linlithgow Festival Trust. (Picture by kind permission of Thom Pollock)

Opposite: While its waters no longer power Linlithgow's industries, the River Avon still provides an attractive setting for the town's Bridge Inn, one of the many businesses in the town that makes it a delightful place for visitors to come. As is always remembered on Marches morning, the bridge over the Avon marks the town's western boundary with what was formerly Stirlingshire, and now comes under the authority of Falkirk Unitary Council. (Picture by kind permission of John Doherty)

The palace wine cellar provided the substitute setting for the marriage of the young Mary Queen of Scots to Francis Dauphin of France in Notre Dame Cathedral, Paris, when it was re-enacted in August 1996 by members of the Linlithgow Festival Trust. (Picture by kind permission of Thom Pollock)

In his role as Grand Prior, Thom Pollock led the royal procession through the courtyard with his daughter Victoria playing the role of the teenage Mary Queen of Scots. (Picture by kind permission of Thom Pollock)

The entrance to the Lyon Chalmer banqueting hall of the palace provided a suitable vantage point for these spectators on this sunny August Sunday afternoon in 1994. (Picture by kind permission of Thom Pollock)

On her way to her execution, Mary Queen of Scots, played this time by Victoria's mother, Clare Pollock, pauses to glance at the plaque on the wall of Linlithgow's Kirk Gate, which now records her tragic life. The young courtier in the picture is Kerry Jamieson and the Lady In Waiting, Elma Martin. (Picture by kind permission of Thom Pollock)

The entire cast of the drama about the life of Mary Queen of Scots posed for the photographer in front of the largest fireplace in Scotland in the magnificent banqueting hall in Linlithgow Palace. It was in this splendid setting that the famous Scottish play *Ane Satyre of the Thrie Estatis* by Sir David Lyndsay was first performed before the court of King James V as the climax to the Christmas celebrations on the Twelfth Night, 6 January 1540. Lest the clergy in the audience in the Great Hall that night had failed to grasp the point of the play, King James himself is said to have added to it by addressing them all at the close of the performance. Sadly, it was to no avail and twenty years later the Reformation took place in 1560. (Picture by kind permission of Thom Pollock)

While Sir David Lyndsay made his mark in Scotland, south of the border in England it was Shakespeare who ruled the stage. A *Midsummer Night's Dream* was one of the Bard's most successful comedies and the rose garden made a perfect rustic setting for it when the Linlithgow Players presented the play on 23 June 1994. (Picture by kind permission of Thom Pollock)

Moving forward two centuries from the days of Shakespeare, there were the visits of Mary Queen of Scots and John Knox to Linlithgow Palace. Prince Charles Edward Stuart, the Young Pretender, also visited the palace on his triumphant march south to Edinburgh at the start of the Jacobite Uprising in 1745, an occasion also re-enacted by the members of the town's festival trust. (Picture by kind permission of Thom Pollock)

Hop Scotch is the title for the series of open air dances which John Carsewell organizes on Wednesday evenings during late July and early August in the palace courtyard. While concentrating on audience participation in Scottish reels, jigs, strathspeys and other traditional dances, visiting groups of dancers from other countries are often invited to give displays of their national dances as happened on this occasion in July 1995 when these enthusiastic young people from Romania visited the town.

While Linlithgow welcomes groups of young people, especially from Guyencourt, its twin town in France, its own youngsters also on occasion travel beyond the Burgh boundaries to display their talents. On this occasion Duncan Russell as Hans Christian Andersen led the cast of Linlithgow Primary School's production of *The Ugly Duckling* in an alfresco performance in Edinburgh's Parliament Square as part of the capital's Danish Festival in May 1993. David Laing played the part of the top hatted circus proprietor, Phineas T. Barnum.

Before West Lothian County Cricket Club acquired its ground at Boghall in the spring of 1930, matches were played regularly on the grass of the Peel. Local legend still fondly recalls the day when the mighty Bamberry, the town halberdier and bell ringer, hit one ball so far it landed against the palace wall. Other hazards faced by similar big hitters, such as Councillors Jimmy Borthwick and David Morrison, included a huge tree near the wicket and the loch, where a boat was kept to rescue balls that landed in the water. David Morrison is second from right in the front row, next to Scottish international Sandy Paris, holding the bat. Cricketing names remembered with fond affection in Linlithgow include those of club professional Charlie Benham, his sons, Fred, Maurice and Arthur, Andrew and John Raeburn, George Strachan, Jim Shanks, and Alec Ford and his sons Malcolm and Donald, the latter of whom also played for Hearts and was capped for Scotland. Boghall is now frequently chosen for Scottish international matches. On these occasions the town is often lucky enough to get a mention on the television weather forecast, perhaps because BBC Scotland's popular 'Heather the Weather' just happens to be the daughter of former West Lothian player Peter Reid.

Nine

Linlithgow at School

Learning in Linlithgow stretches back through the centuries to the days of the Sang Scule in the Kirk Gate, first mentioned in 1187. There the priests of St Michael's church taught the choirboys singing and basic academic lessons. By the time of the Reformation, when John Knox in his First Book of Discipline recommended a school in every parish, Linlithgow already had its well-established grammar school. Its rector was the able Ninian Winzet, who debated with Knox, and who when forced for religious reasons to leave Scotland, proved capable enough to go on to become Bishop of Ratisbon in Germany. A century later Linlithgow had an equally controversial schoolmaster, Alexander Kirkwood, author of the famous *Kirkwood's Latin Grammar*, who was again sufficiently learned, and a free thinker to defy the dictates of his employers, the provost, bailies and magistrates. Sarcastically, he dubbed them the 'Twenty-seven Gods of Linlithgow!' During the seventeenth century Linlithgow was thought highly enough of as a place of learning to be a suitable temporary home for the students of the University of Edinburgh. The students were forced to flee the city because of an outbreak of plague and came instead to attend lectures in St Michael's Kirk. It is appropriate therefore that Linlithgow still has a reputation for its good schools which attract many families to come to live in the town. At the primary stage there are four schools, Linlithgow Primary, Lowport, Springfield and St Josephs. The largest is the three-stream Linlithgow Primary. It was founded in 1844 by the congregation of the town's new Free Church, formed the previous year as a result of the Disruption of the Church of Scotland. To begin with, the pupils were taught on weekdays in the same pews of the church, where the worshippers gathered on Sundays. They were also summoned to their classes by the Kirk bell, which can still be seen outside the main entrance to the school's modern premises in Preston Road. In 1872 the Scottish Education Act brought Linlithgow Public School under the control of the town's newly established School Board. At first it provided both primary education and some secondary schooling in the form of supplementary classes for those pupils whose parents allowed them to stay on beyond the statutory leaving age of twelve years. In 1894, the School Board decided to open Linlithgow Academy in what is now Longcroft Hall at West Port. It was originally a fee paying school and when it opened had only seventeen pupils, thirteen girls and four boys, who were taught by Headmaster Alexander Muir MA, and Assistant Mistress Miss Maggie McLaren. A few free scholarships were offered and soon the number of pupils increased to sixty-five. In November, Mr John Charles Will was appointed as the school's first male assistant teacher. By May 1900, when the Academy pupils were given an extra holiday to commemorate the British victory in South Africa over the Boers at Mafeking, there was extra cause for celebration – the School Board announced that larger premises were to be constructed at Low Port. Designed in an attractive Scottish baronial style by well-known church architect Grahame Fairley, the new school took two years to complete at a cost of £7,000. When it opened it had one hundred and two pupils under its first rector, James Beveridge, who was assisted by seven teachers. The Academy continued in its beautiful setting at Low Port with games often enjoyed on the lawns of the adjacent Peel until 1967, when it moved to its present site at Braehead. There could not have been a greater contrast, an entry in the school magazine describing the ugly modern new premises as, 'dominated by a slaughter house, a cemetery, the rooftops of Braehead, and a railway.' The Academy's loss was Low Port Primary School's gain as, after a short period when they were used as Council offices, the school took over the Edwardian buildings. As Linlithgow continued to grow from a population of under 4,000 in 1945 to one of over 14, 000 in 1995, it was decided that the town required a further primary school, and the open-plan Springfield opened in the centre of the housing estate of the same name at the east end of the town. Pupils from Springfield, Low Port and Linlithgow Primary go onto secondary education at Linlithgow Academy, while those from St Josephs, which was founded as long ago as 1889, travel out of the town to attend St Kentigerns in Blackburn.

Rector, staff and pupils marched along Linlithgow High Street to take possession of the newly completed Linlithgow Academy, complete with its turrets and roof top cupola, when it was ready for occupation in 1902. This picture shows it in that year. The building's fine stone work was the work of James Hardie and Sons of Bo'ness, and the joinery work was done by A. Bathgate and Son of Linlithgow. At the right hand door can be seen several of the lady members of staff, including Lady Superintendent Miss Annie Murray, Miss Emma Morris and Miss I. Roberts, who taught the girls domestic science. Equally sexist was the fact that all of the women on the staff were single as the rules of the Linlithgow School Board decreed that they must resign their posts upon marriage! (Picture by kind permission of Jim Shanks)

The Academy's familiar turreted towers framed the senior pupils of the 1945 to 1946 school session, when they posed for this group photograph along with their rector, Mr William Baxter, and teachers Mr William 'Billy' Burt and the famous Miss Gladys Meek. The pupils are from left to right, back row: Jim Shanks, Harry Mercer, David Bissett, Sandy Bannerman. Middle row: Dorothy Porteous, Dorothy Thompson, Isobel Lawrie, Sheena Dick-Smith, Shelagh Scott. Front row: Sydnet Smyth, Mabel Gray, David Cook, John (Mike) Allan. (Picture by kind permission of Jim Shanks)

Around the same year, the Academy's senior cricket team consisted of, from left to right, back row: William Jowett, Gordon Black, Jim Currie, Alistair McLean, John Eadie, Jim Fleming, Fraser Drummond, David Stein. Front row: Harry Merker, Sandy Bannerman, David Cook (Team Captain), Sydney Smyth, Jim Shanks. Seated in front: Austen Sharp (Scorer). (Picture by kind permission of Jim Shanks)

As the sign proclaims, this photograph shows the girls of Linlithgow Academy's First XI Hockey team in their navy gym tunics at the end of the 1950s. They include Pat Bowe, Janette Lockhart, Kathleen McMaster, Davina Mitchell, Dorothy Muir, Agnes Watson and Betty Wood.

Art Advisor Bill Thomson looks on proudly at the opening of the 1981 Edinburgh Festival Art Exhibition. Linlithgow Academy was represented at the ceremony by John Ferguson (Rector), Jimmy Dewar (Principal Teacher of Art), Bobby Monaghan (Assistant Art Teacher), Kay Fleming (Head Girl), and in the centre of the photograph, art pupil Margot Thomson, several pieces of whose work had been selected for display. The popular art advisor had particular reason for feeling proud on this occasion, as Margot is his daughter. Like her father she has since gone on to make art her career and has gained recognition for her designs for the internationally famous Caithness Glass Company in Perth.

The Linlithgow Academy's former Edwardian premises are now home to the two hundred pupils of Low Port Primary. During its thirty year existence, Low Port has had only two Headteachers, Mr Joe Welsh and his current successor, Mrs C. Cameron. Low Port's Primary One infant pupils in 1996 enjoyed a sunny start to their school days. Here they are posing for the photographer beside the boundary wall of the school's attractive grassy playing field. The school colours are black and gold.

In 1997 Low Port's pupils celebrated the school's harvest festival by staging a fancy dress parade. Included in this photograph are Hannah Thomson, Eleanor Wigham, Tom Sneddon, Lucy McLaughlin, Rachel Wilson, Thomas Walton and Andrew Goudie.

During the same year the pupils of Low Port performed the school show *Lost Little Kitten*. Here they are seen performing the Snow Drop Dance. They inlcude Jenna McColm, Katherine Thompson, Matthew Rowe, David Sote, Luke Quigley, Hayley Smith and Alexander Chadwick.

113

Low Port pupils Sam Best and Calum Robertson enjoyed a chat with this papier mâché model of Grandpa, when they met in 1995. The school badge on the sweatshirt depicts the school's initials enclosed in laurel leaves.

Low Port pupils often go on project outings including this exciting one to Blackness Castle in 1997. Children in the photograph include Ryan Williams, Claire Williamson, Gordon Cormacle and Rory Little, who were all pupils of Primary Five.

Another regular popular outing is to the West Lothian Country Park at Beecraigs. Here, the 1996 Primary One class confidently asked questions of the countryside rangers, watched by their teacher Miss Paxton, who before retiring had taught at Low Port for twenty years.

Low Port is also strong on sports and this photograph taken in 1992 shows the school cricket team. These enthusiastic young players captured top Scottish honours by winning the national short cricket tournament held on the inches at Perth, as well as several other cups and trophies, which augurs well for the future of the game in West Lothian.

Outdoor education also features in the well-varied curriculum at Low Port, and here the school's pupils are about to embark on a sailing lesson on the loch under the ever watchful eye of the fully qualified instructors from the neighbouring Low Port Centre. The outdoor centre, under manager George Thomson and bursar Mrs Maggie Wilson, offers residential courses for up to thirty-eight participants and activities available include canoeing, kayaking, rafting, wind surfing, all-terrain biking, orienteering and problem solving. During term time priority is given to pupils from West Lothian schools, but at other times of the year bookings are considered from different organizations.

Springfield Primary School was well represented at Linlithgow and Linlithgow Bridge Gala Day in 1995, with young Christopher Ball on his tricycle, despite his severe physical handicaps, proudly leading the parade of decorated bikes. Headteacher Mrs Alison McAllan is pictured on the right.

The school chose the theme of world travel for its decorated cycles in the Gala Day parade.

Springfield Primary's smartly uniformed pupils enjoy a section of the school playground, which is especially set aside for quiet games. The school colour is green. The girls in the centre of the picture enjoying the games provided by the school's Parent Teacher Association are Karen Lochtie and Fiona MacFarlane.

Brass music instructress Lorraine Bisson conducted this carol rehearsal in one of Springfield Primary School's classrooms, its walls decorated with the pupils' project work. The young players are, from left to right: Peter Togneri, Erin Fairley and 1997 Junior Musician of the Year Kirsty Lindsay.

Grant Kerr and other Springfield Primary School pupils enjoyed taking part in a science investigation in their classroom during the 1997 school year.

Springfield Primary School pupils David Convoy, Isla McLennan, Paval Uppal and Andrew Robinson enjoyed trying their hand at being pavement artists in the school playground during the summer of 1996.

Pupils from Springfield Primary regularly take part in road safety exercises. This photograph shows them practising their kerb drill under the watchful eye of a constable from Lothian and Borders Police on the pavement of Springfield Road outside the school.

Following up on their school concert which had a conservation theme, Springfield pupils entered this colourfully decorated tableau in the 1998 Linlithgow and Linlithgow Bridge Gala Day procession, seen here passing the former St Michaels Hotel, which has now been converted into flats overlooking the High Street.

St Joseph's Primary pupils took each other's fingerprints during this lesson in one of the school's modern classrooms. In the background, even the classroom doll wears a St Joseph's scarlet and white tie. The equally smartly uniformed real life pupils are Siobhan Coleman, Rachael Tierney, James Doherty, Michael Walker, Ross Green, Lindsay Banks and Madeline Chessar.

Ruth McLoughlin, Laura Meahan, Lauren Boyle, Fiona Porteous and Mark Lambert enjoy taking part in a science investigation at St Joseph's Primary School.

Art lessons at St Joseph's Primary School are always fun as was the case with this particular lesson in which Alasdair Robertson, Paul McLean, Sean Higgins, Neil Gallacher and Emily Aitken made black bats for Hallowe'en.

Making paper mâché is always an enjoyably messy activity as these St Joseph's Primary pupils Gillian Porteous, Andrew McGinniss and Douglas Coyle happily discovered during this art lesson.

School does, however, also have its more serious side as illustrated by this busy group of pupils when the photographer visited their classroom. Facing the camera are, from left to right: Neil Gallacher, Rachel Farmer and Emma Connor.

Christmas is always a very special time of year at St Joseph's Primary School. Here the boys and girls are pictured enjoying the many treats on offer at a festive tea party.

St Joseph's pupils with their model ships.

Linlithgow Primary School's thick sandstone-walled West Port building stands on the site where the school was founded in 1844. Nicknamed 'Colditz' by generations of pupils, the old school looks Victorian but was actually erected during the first few years of the twentieth century. The glass-canopied roof of the assembly hall was designed to open so that when pupils took part in physical education exercises they could enjoy fresh air. Attempts to close West Port have been made by the local education authority since the 1960s but it will still house classes at the Millenium, and this historic building is regarded with great affection by both former pupils and staff.

In marked contrast this picture shows Linlithgow Primary School's 1967 building, photographed from the main entrance in Preston Road. The flat-roofed building has all of the architectural defects of a school designed in the 1960s and has weathered the years badly in comparison with the school's West Port building. The Preston Road building shares a campus with St Joseph Primary and Linlithgow Academy. The site also has the capacity to house all of the school's 750 pupils if West Lothian Council's Education Department has the will to do so, rather than continuing its campaign to reduce the roll and build an additional single-stream school somewhere in the Linlithgow Bridge area of the town.

Linlithgow Primary led the way amongst British schools in welcoming parents to share in its activities, including participating in worship at its morning assemblies. Its pioneering work was featured in the television series *Parents In School*. In this photograph pupils proudly display their house shields (from left to right: Bruce, Douglas, Stewart and Wallace) as Headmaster William F. Hendrie announced the points gained for good work and behaviour during the previous week.

Pupils relaxed on the grass on the school playing field at Preston Road during this sports day in the early 1980s. The high wall separates the playing field from the Union Canal, which flows above it. In the background, on the far side of the canal, can be seen the raked roofs of the houses of the Deanburn Estate, one of the first to be built on the hillside above the town. The young families who lived in the estate helped to swell the role of Linlithgow Primary in the 1970s, making it the largest primary school in the country.

Outdoor environmental education was one of the many strengths of the well-balanced curriculum at Linlithgow Primary. Here, Primary Seven pupils were about to set out for a night exploration walk during a residential week at Benmore Outdoor Education Centre on the Cowal Peninsula near Dunoon. Benmore, Lagganlia near Aviemore in the Highlands, and Dalguise in Pethshire also accommodated the school's innovative and highly successful annual parent and pupil weekends.

Jacqueline Cummings, Neil Mowat, Elizabeth Bowen, David Grant, Siobhan Harvey and Janet Smyth were among the Linlithgow Primary pupils who took part in the school's Burns Supper, televised by Scottish Television for the award-winning programme *Wi' Best Respekts*

Glen Michael's Cavalcade Christmas and New Year Specials were televised from Linlithgow Primary School by Scottish Television. In this photograph the popular entertainer is seen talking on stage with the show's floor manager, while the members of the school choir waited to perform. The girl in the feather boa is Nikki Craig, who went on to enjoy a successful career in the world of entertainment and is now running a health and leisure complex in Malta. Nikki still keeps in close touch with her family and friends in her hometown.

One of Linlithgow Primary's most famous former pupils is internationally renowned classical concert pianist Stephen Osborne. Here, Stephen is seen making his television debut when Scotland's top children's entertainer Glen Michael featured him on his televised show from the Preston Road assembly hall of the school. Another of the school's old boys is Alex Salmond, leader of the Scottish National Party, who took part in his first ever election campaign when Linlithgow Primary staged a mock election to coincide with the General Election in 1964. Thirty-five years later in the 1999 run up to the first Scottish Parliamentary Election, Salmond recalled the event when he took part in BBC Radio Four's *Any Questions* programme. He told listeners his schoolboy manifesto included the proposed replacement of lukewarm school milk at mid-morning playtime with Cabrelli's ice cream! This novel idea obviously swayed the young voters because young Alex won the election for the Scots Nats, of course!

Linlithgow Primary School's unique palace junior guides were recognized by the Scottish Tourist Board when they helped the town win this tourism Oscar. The Oscar is seen here being presented by West Lothian County Convener Councillor Jimmy McGinley to Headmaster William F. Hendrie, Deputy Head Margaret Mackay and Primary Seven pupils Susan Farrow, Robert Lee and Rowan Dick. This was a success, which particularly delighted Jimmy McGinley. As well as being West Lothian's civic leader, he was also Linlithgow Primary School's janitor, and always took a keen interest in the progress of its pupils. Jimmy often took part in the school's debating society, 'Talk Shop', sat in on rehearsals for school shows and attended the resultant performances. He also gave great encouragement to the school's multi-award winning newspaper *Primary Press*, which won *The Scotsman* school newspaper competition on numerous occasions and *The Times* school newspaper competition several times. *Primary Press*'s biggest scoop was interviewing Prime Minister Margaret Thatcher.

Linlithgow Primary School's annual musical productions were always famed for their casts of hundreds as can be seen from this photograph of principals and chorus from the 1986 production of *Make Me A World*, pictured against the backdrop designed and painted by Barbara Braithwaite. Barbara was also stage manager for most of the school's other colourful productions, which included *Alice In Wonderland*, *The Wizard of Oz*, *Twist*, *Tom Sawyer*, *The Ugly Duckling*, *Wee MacGreegor*, *The Playground War*, *Anne of Green Gables*, *Land of Counterpane*, *Pinocchio* and *The Jungle Book*. (Picture by kind permission of Tempest)